3 Steps to a Strong Family

LINDA and RICHARD EYRE

With Contributions from Their Children

Simon & Schuster

New York   London   Toronto   Sydney   Tokyo   Singapore

SIMON & SCHUSTER
Rockefeller Center
1230 Avenue of the Americas
New York, New York 10020

Designed by Irving Perkins Associates

Manufactured in the United States of America

10 9 8 7 6 5 4 3 2 1

Library of Congress Cataloging-in-Publication Data is available.

ISBN: 0-671-88728-9

Contents

There are three key reasons for setting up a basic family legal system, a simple, child-involving economy, and some fun traditions. First, they'll help you prepare your children for the real world. Second, they'll help you keep your sanity—and enjoy your family more. Third, they'll help you give your children a sense of values, consistency, and security in a time when all three are harder and harder to find.

The three steps *work*. But don't try to do them all at once. Be sure to tailor them to your own situation and needs. And don't expect instant results.

It's the law you want your children to learn to obey, not the people. "Because I said so" is not nearly as good an answer as "because it's the law we discussed and that we've agreed will make us happier."

Simple, clear rules or limits that result from parents' love give children a security that "no limit" kids secretly yearn for. These limits also teach self-discipline and respect, and they actually expand children's independence.

A simple family legal structure involves three things: family laws, penalties for breaking laws, and a way to "repent" and thus avoid punishment.

Laws or rules cannot govern all behavior, so children also need to make *good decisions*—and to make certain key decisions *in advance.*

Review how feasible the plot is before you continue. Remind yourself that everything takes time, every child and every family is unique, there are no "parenting experts," and a sense of humor is the best tool of all.

Step 2
Paying Your Dues:

An economic system not only provides money, goods, and services, it also fosters motivation, discipline, and self-reliance. It creates ownership through which people take responsibility and care for their things. It allows people to save, to work toward goals. It also gives individuals opportunities to help each other.

Many families have economic systems that children can't participate in. Many others have a somewhat counterproductive system called allowances, which may teach the dangerous notion of something for nothing.

A good family economy disciplines and enriches parents even as it teaches children decision-making, delayed gratification, future planning, empathy, goal-setting, and dependability.

A simple family economy involves three things: a way for children to earn money, an incentive to save money, and the opportunity to learn to spend money responsibly.

Put yourself in the play—can it work for you? Realize that *every* parent feels frustration, guilt, inadequacy—and that while love is often easy, time and patience usually aren't.

Step 3
Making Magic:

Traditions give an institution permanence and pride—and give identity and solid codes of behavior to its members.

Most families have traditions already, ranging from things they do on holidays or birthdays to how they communicate with each other.

But when traditions are carefully thought out; formalized a little; put on a calendar; looked forward to; talked about afterward; and built upon over the years, they can bond a family; increase loyalty; open up whole new realms of communication; teach lessons about faith, respect, honesty, and service; and bring families back together often, even years after children have left home. The best family traditions teach or reinforce *values*.

You should use this section as a recipe book. Pick out the courses that appeal to you, find the ingredients, and make them happen.

Or, for a single parent, better relationships and better teamwork with others who love and care for your child.

Working together on the same goal, the same hope, the same project draws people closer than anything else. Children are our hope; their happiness should be our goal, and they are certainly a *project!*

Raising a happy child who can cope with today's world and creating a family that becomes a lasting institution are life's most demanding challenges. There is no easy formula or set of pat answers. But the challenges yield to commitment, to effort, to never giving up. The results come slowly and gradually—but with joy. And the results can change the world . . . one family at a time.

Beyond the benefits to parents and to individual households, strong families can save this country. Children are our most important stewardship, and the social problems that are ripping America apart can only be solved by parents within families.

What it is and how to join.

Acknowledgments

We feel special appreciation for the fifty thousand parents who make up HOMEBASE, our worldwide parents' organization, and their input and support for our work; our synergistic editor, Ed Walters, and others at Simon & Schuster who are such a pleasure to work with; our vastly capable and loyal personal assistant, typist, and alter ego Corry DeMille; Stephen Covey, whose foreword reflects the generosity of his life; and most of all, our own nine children, who helped us write this book and who are the reason we cared enough to write it.

Foreword

Leo Tolstoy said: "All happy families are alike; every unhappy family is unhappy in its own way." What did he
mean? Certainly, there are many different causes for un-
happiness in families—but in what way are happy families
the same?

The strong and happy families of all nationalities,
creeds, ethnic, and religious backgrounds are rooted in
living universal principles that produce the fruit of love
and trust. Happy, strong families are principle-centered.

Linda and Richard Eyre have discovered three essential
elements that are common among happy families—three
steps through which parents can build loyalty and love
and establish patterns that lead to strong and enduring
families.

This is a tremendously hope-filled and optimistic book
that says no matter what your economic-social situation
and no matter where you live, there are three basic steps,
doable by *any* parent, that can strengthen your family.

The Eyres' previous best-seller, *Teaching Your Children
Values*, gave parents a practical "menu" of methods for
teaching values. Now their "3 Steps" help parents to raise
happier, more secure and responsible children and promote more open communication in families. Through their
exemplary family, practical writings and presentations, remarkable public service, and the international organization of parents (HOMEBASE has over 50,000 members),
Linda and Richard Eyre are making a tremendous contri-

11

bution to society's most basic and important institution—
the family. I admire them enormously. What a team!

Stephen R. Covey
Chairman, Covey Leadership Center
Author, *The 7 Habits of Highly Effective People*
and *Principle-Centered Leadership*

Prelude

Building a family and raising children are life's most important opportunity—and its most difficult challenge. But families don't come with instruction manuals or owner's handbooks. Where can parents turn for advice on building a stronger, happier family? Right here—the book in your hands. We've come to realize that building a working family doesn't have to be an impossible or overwhelming task. It doesn't require an advanced degree in family "engineering," and it doesn't mean reading every book written by experts on the family.

It does require understanding the three elements that all successful and enduring institutions share, and then building on and encouraging these elements in our own families—through three simple steps that are doable by families of every size and shape and from every kind of background.

Think about it for a minute. No institution, from a club to a school to a country, works very well or lasts very long without three things:

- Rules or laws (a legal system)
- A way of allocating resources (an economy)
- Strong traditions based on shared values

A family, the most basic and essential of all institutions, requires all three. To be happy, united, and lasting, a family needs:

1. A legal system: fair, consistent discipline based on rules and limits
2. An economy: a way for children to earn, save, and spend money
3. Traditions: family activities that build communication, trust, and togetherness

These are the "3 steps" of this book. Together, they form the infrastructure of a strong family. Think about the word *infrastructure*—it means the systems that hold something together, that make it work. A city's infrastructure might be its roads, its bridges, its water and power lines. A corporation's infrastructure could be its lines of organization—who reports to whom, who is responsible for what duties, how decisions get made, and how things get done. *Infra* means *under* or *below*; *infrastructure* is the structure below the surface that makes it possible for everything else to function.

When it breaks down—think of a power line breaking, or a road with potholes—the failure of infrastructure can be stressful, waste your time, and lead to a host of related problems that can be difficult to fix.

Today many families lack a good infrastructure—that is to say, they lack basic reliable *systems* that can help govern behavior and help children communicate and stay connected and united, even as they are learning to be unique individuals. Without these underpinnings children may feel lost, and parents may find themselves overwhelmed by family problems and demands.

This book is about the three steps that can create a basic family infrastructure that will help you use your limited time more effectively, reduce the inherent stress of raising

14

a family, and help you teach your children the values they need.

So many of the things we'd like to teach our children and to have as part of our family life—such as open communication, strong relationships, a sense of responsibility, good personal judgment, warm and happy times together—are hard to *impose* on a family. You can't just walk in one day and announce, "Today, we're going to communicate more," or "Let's have a warm, fuzzy family moment *now*."

"Experts" can teach us techniques—of throwing and catching, for example—but without a ball these methods are meaningless, not to mention tiring and a little silly. Having an expert explain the psychological theory behind discipline or a philosophy of moral values doesn't help parents who are facing real problems, real challenges, with their children. Knowing the communications techniques we should be using won't do us much good unless we have something to talk about.

What parents need are ways of making these things happen naturally. With children it's very important to offer tangible subjects they can be interested in and communicate about, meaningful responsibilities they can learn from, significant decisions they can make, and genuine situations that can deepen their relationship with their family and cause everyone to love being together.

This book is about real, concrete activities you can use to create an atmosphere in your home that will ensure that the things that are important to you—discipline, responsibility, communication, sharing—happen naturally. This family infrastructure of a legal system, an economy, and traditions doesn't take the place of sensitivity or understanding; it can't substitute for communication or love. But it does provide a framework that helps these happen, in the same way that electricity flows over power lines or goods are delivered over a city's roads. And it creates an atmosphere that provides more natural opportunities for that elusive thing we call quality time with our children.

Every home, whether its occupants recognize it or not, has some form of legal system, economy, and traditions. In many families these have developed in a haphazard and almost unconscious way. This kind of infrastructure can be counterproductive for our children, and a tremendous drain on our time. If our "legal system" is inconsistent, for example, if the rules keep changing, it is almost inevitable that our children will be rebellious and misbehaving. If the family's finances are handled poorly, and children have no opportunity to earn money or learn about it, there are bound to be constant disagreements about how it's spent—on clothes, school, entertainment, and so forth. And if the family can't rely on good traditions to bring them together—or if the traditions the family does have reinforce bad habits or behavior—stress and frustration increase and family members drift apart.

This book is about making your rules, finances, and traditions work for you; about making them real, tangible parts of the life you share with your children; about using them as opportunities to teach your children about communication, responsibility, and decision making. It offers you a "ball" to "put in play"—specific suggestions that can help you give your family more order and more purpose, while you reduce the stress you feel as a parent.

Setting up a family infrastructure takes time, but it will end up saving you time in two ways. First, within a simple

but solid family legal and economic system children become more self-reliant and independent, learning principles that will help them govern themselves—saving
parents time (and trouble). Second, good systems and
good traditions provide the security and promote the communication that helps keep families together longer, giving parents more time in which to nurture their children
and help them become good people, good citizens, and
eventually good parents themselves.

In a world full of frustrations, where we often feel pow-
erless to change anything, how reassuring it can be to
realize that you *can* change and improve the thing that
matters most, that affects society the most, that fulfills you
the most—your family!

As much as peers, the media, and schools may influence our children, there are ways that we as parents can
be an even greater influence. This involves taking the initiative, taking advantage of our unique relationship with
our child or children to create a basic plan for building and
strengthening our family, rather than just hoping we'll
know how to react when our children have problems.

The main purpose of this book is to show you how to
develop a plan for your family. The three steps will work
for families of all sizes, and with children of all ages. As
you read the book, you'll recognize specific suggestions
that seem natural for your situation. Pick out the ones that
will work the best for you and adapt them to suit the ages
of your children. While it's never too late to start building
a stronger family through the three steps, it works best if
you start early. Most of the methods and suggestions in
this book are designed for use with children between the
ages of three and twelve with the "epicenter" for many

ideas being age *eight*—a rather miraculous time when children are quick and conceptual, flattered and complimented by responsibility, and not yet cynical or hormone driven.

One way in which this book is unusual is that we and our children wrote it as a family. Throughout the book you'll find comments, reactions, and feedback from our children, who have actually experienced and tested the suggestions we're making. Often the children's insights were clearer and more realistic than our own. The children are after all the reason for these three steps.

The children's comments are entirely their own. We showed them an outline of what we wanted to write about and asked them for their comments. (Actually we *showed* it to four of our boys—Jonah, sixteen years old; Talmadge, fourteen; Noah, twelve; and Eli, ten. We *read* it to Charity, seven, and *sent* it to Saren, twenty-three; Shawni, twenty-one; and Josh, nineteen, who are doing humanitarian service and missionary work in Bulgaria, Romania, and England, respectively, and to Saydi, eighteen, who is a college student near Boston.) Their entries are pretty much unedited—even the spelling—and, like some of our own personal comments, are set off in a different typeface.

Also, since our family's size and composition is not typical (indeed, *no* family type is typical anymore because there are so many family types), we drew inputs from our vast parents' network HOMEBASE*—some 50,000 families throughout the world, including every conceivable type of family, *all* of which can benefit from the same three steps.

---

* HOMEBASE is an international co-op of parents. See last section of book for details.

As you read this book, don't get the idea that things always work out as smoothly as they might seem from these entries. Remember, we wrote the book—and in most cases we've picked out our best memories. Please don't view us as *experts*. Think of us as fellow strugglers. We couldn't put in all of our mistakes or frustrations because we didn't want to end up with a thousand-page book. Parenting is a difficult business—and different for each of us. The only person who can be an expert on your child is you.

May the three steps work for all of us. May they be the gifts of survival and success that we give to our children.

Linda and Richard Eyre
McLean, Virginia
Winter 1994

Overture

It's nice, before getting deeply into any program of music, to hear a little overture—a little sampling of the music—as a way of getting in the right mood and becoming prepared and receptive for what is to come. So reflect with us for a few minutes about what we're going to be talking about, about the nature of families, and about why these "three steps" deserve serious consideration.

—Linda

The interesting thing about being a parent is that what we're really trying to do is work our way out of the job. We're aiming to get our children to a point where they can govern themselves, where they are law-abiding citizens who can handle their own money, live by good values, and become parents capable of passing the same abilities, morality, and basic happiness on to their own children (our grandchildren).

The world around us, complete with all its media and peer pressure, offers up all kinds of irresponsible models, unethical examples, and amoral behavior. So we as parents look for ways of making the most basic institution— our homes—a microcosm of the *best* the world has to offer: a place of thoughtful obedience to good laws, responsible stewardship over the material things we have earned, and a safe harbor of unconditional love and unifying traditions.

But the *ways* in which we try to do so had better be simple and workable, because we are *busy*. And it is stressful trying to find time for family and to balance our children's needs with our work and personal needs.

What we don't need is a bunch of psychobabble or advice from parenting "experts." Parenting has become a science, or an art, or a field of study—or so one would think by looking at all of the books, articles, advice, methods, techniques, and programs being offered up these days. Too often parents are intimidated, wondering how they could ever succeed at such an incredibly complex task without the benefit of advanced psychology degrees. Other parents are put on guilt trips, realizing how they do so few of the things that "experts" say they should and how many things they do that experts say they shouldn't. Still other parents (perhaps most) just aren't involved with the "expertise" at all—not reading any of the books or studying and applying the techniques because they simply don't have any left-over time or energy.

There are whole volumes of theory about time management, about communication techniques, and about positive reinforcement for parents. But what we need is a workable lifestyle and some patterns or habits in our homes that foster *natural* rather than forced communications, that give us frequent *natural* opportunities for praising positive behavior, and that get kids doing the things we want them to do in more *natural* ways without us forever reminding and enforcing them.

We went through periods when we did read the "expert parenting" books, felt the intimidation and the guilt; at other times we were too busy or too frustrated. Somewhere along

22

the line we got just critical and cynical enough to decide that no parenting advice was any good at all unless it reduced our own stress and helped us enjoy our children more. We defined a good parenting idea as one that saved us time instead of adding to our juggling act; improved communication and brought us closer to our kids rather than distancing them from us; and involved positive ideas that built our kids up, not critical, exacting, judgmental, negative ones.

—Richard

What we need to do is to get down to bedrock basics. How can we create a home that works efficiently, that provides security and identity, and that turns initiative over to the children and prepares them for the real world?

That is the *question*. Taking the three steps of setting up a family legal system, economy, and traditions is the *answer*—an answer that promotes peace, order, and communication in the home.

But to do so takes some time—and some commitment—so as parents we need to be *clear* on just exactly *why* we are doing it. Being clear about the "why" gives us the motivation and incentive to stick with it. And more important than the time and stress we save ourselves is what we can do for our children. In that sense there are at least three extremely basic reasons for trying the three steps—setting up a legal system, an economy, and a series of good traditions in your family:

- They'll help you prepare your children for the real world.
- They'll help you keep your sanity—and enjoy your family more.

- They'll help you give your children a sense of values, consistency, and security in a time when all three are getting harder and harder to find.

Let's review each of these reasons in our overture—before the curtain goes up:

WHY #1: *The three steps will help prepare your children for both the positive and the negative realities of the outside world.*

In the real world there are laws—laws of nature, laws of government, laws of God—and when we break them, we face a penalty or punishment unless we repent or can make restitution. In the real world people get ahead or fall behind according to how hard they work, how much they save, the choices they make. And in the real world our habits, attitudes, and the way we approach things determine how happy we are and how happy we make other people.

The world our children go out into today is a scary place indeed, especially for kids. Sixteen thousand crimes are committed on or near school property every day. One hundred thirty-five thousand students carry guns to school. One in seven teens say they have tried to commit suicide. Forty percent of today's fourteen-year-old girls will become pregnant by the time they are nineteen. "Moral reasoning" has replaced "character education" in schools, and safe sex has become doctrine; deviant lifestyles are discussed (as alternatives), and junior-high principals pass out valentines that contain condoms. The average age of first alcohol use has dropped to 12.3 years.

Six out of ten high school seniors say they have used illegal drugs. Violent crime in America has increased by 580 percent over three decades, and rape by 42 percent in one decade.

Enough time has passed since the "permissive parenting" and skyrocketing divorce rates of the sixties, seventies, and eighties that conclusive data on the results are in. Kids from broken families are at far higher risk for drugs, teen pregnancy, dropping out of school, and suicide. Juvenile problems that spill out of the family and become social problems cost society a fortune and are rarely solved.

A good home should help prepare a child to cope with these realities. If kids grow up without the security of rules or limits in their families, they will break the rules and ignore the limits of society. If they are bribed with allowances, gifts, and privileges, they may go into the world expecting to get something for nothing or looking for the kind of have-now-pay-later instant gratification that destroys so many people. And if they have no traditions to look forward to, they may enter into their adult lives without the good memories, good habits, and good values they need to survive in our society.

As Confucius said, "Let families take care of families and society will take care of itself!" To take the thought a step farther, children whose homes teach them correct principles will be able to face the world and make it a better place.

Our daughter Saydi puts it in perspective:

I'm in my first year at college and living away from home for the first time. The unique ways our family operates makes me

25

extra homesick. I have a lot of specific things to miss but I'm realizing that they have also prepared me in many ways for living on my own in the wild world. Just little things that I never really thought about before have made it so much easier to make the transition into being on my own. For example, when I was eight and I received my first checkbook for our family bank, I was excited because I could be like Mommy, but now I realize that having that responsibility that early helps me now to understand the value of money and how to budget and spend carefully when i have no back-up at all. I watch some of my new friends who have credit cards with unlimited budgets throw their money away with no sense of responsibility. It makes me feel so good to know that everything I am spending is my own money (earned or borrowed). I think I'm much more appreciative and probably taking more advantage of college. The family jobs helped me prepare for the work *of college.*

Even the family laws I grew up with (though I'm glad to say "good riddance" to some of them—like "asking" before I can go anywhere) have helped me to be organized and to be able to follow the new rules I have to abide by here.

Having family traditions makes it extra hard to be away from home because on Sundays I think about our big family talks and goal-setting times. I get lonesome on birthdays and imagine my family carrying on some tradition I'm missing. Eating at the dorm I got bored without some of our family's crazy "verbal games."

But I will never wish these homesick-causing traditions away—they cause me to be extra proud of my family and have created a bond that will never break. Many people have commented on how they have noticed how much I love and

*appreciate my family and the reason I tell them is because we
have so much fun together.*

—Saydi, 18

WHY #2: *The three steps will help you keep your sanity—
and enjoy your children more.*

We had a friend who was a truly meticulous and absolutely
tenacious parent. She had three children whose rooms were
always in order, who did what she said like privates obeying
a sergeant, who took music lessons and practiced daily, and
who got A's in school.

But the woman was a wreck, and her stress was being
passed along to her children. She took responsibility for everything. It took all day and dozens of reminders, bribes, and
threats to get them to clean up, to practice, to brush their
teeth, to get home on time.

She felt as if everything was working against her—as if she
stood alone against the world and if she let up for a minute,
everything would fall apart.

—Linda

This friend became a model for what we *didn't* want to
be. First because we didn't *have* all day. Second because
we realized that her kids weren't learning anything—she
was taking all the initiative and responsibility in the
family.

The three steps may sound time-consuming, but they
can save you time! It takes time to set up family laws, to
establish a family economy, and to develop family tradi-

tions, but once they're in place, parts of the initiative, incentive, responsibility, and accountability required to keep a family going are *shifted* to your children.

The three steps can also help you reduce the stress level in your family by giving you frequent opportunities to acknowledge your children's good behavior. We all know how important it is to pay attention and reinforce good behavior, but in practice it's incredibly uncommon. Just watch families at any shopping mall and see who's getting all the attention. Naturally it's the kid who's misbehaving.

The basic rules, ways to earn rewards, and consistent family traditions you set up as part of the three steps will give you a chance to replace negative criticism, punishment, and "tearing down" with positive reinforcement, rewards, and "building up."

We've told the story in seminars and speeches around the country, and we've written about it—it seems so simple, but it illustrates so much. It was a rare example of a parent actually ignoring negative behavior and rewarding and being attentive to positive behavior.

The busy mother of three small boys was trying to have a conversation with a neighbor who had come over to borrow a book. The little four-year-old was yelling for her attention and tugging rudely at her skirt. The mother completely ignored the boy until he became so loud that no one else could be heard. Then she casually and matter-of-factly scooped him up like a mop bucket and without even looking at him, and while continuing her conversation with her neighbor, opened the nearest door (it was to a closet), put him behind it, and closed it. Soon he came out, quieted, and politely said, "Excuse me," to get his mother's attention. This time she responded.

The mother ran upstairs to get the book the neighbor wanted. Her other two children were playing together pleasantly. Now she stopped, got down on the floor with them, and said, "You two are playing so nicely with each other and being so kind to each other. . . . I'm so proud of you."

—Richard

Most of us have little trouble finding something to talk about at work, or in our civic roles, or in recreation, because what we are *doing* with other people both requires and invites communication.

In our families what we need is not to try to force or manage communication but to do and share things together that cause us to discuss, to question, to express feelings, and hopefully to listen.

The more you share with your children, the more you'll enjoy them. That's why open, expressive communication is so important to a strong family, and why the three steps are designed to promote it. The bookstores are lined with magazines and books on family communication: "How to talk to your kids," "How to get your kids to talk to you," even "What to talk to your kids about."

I remember an article with that last title—what to talk to your kids about—which suggested that what parents need is something concrete to talk about with their children, something tangible and real, things that have to do with the real world and how it works, things like money and motivation, like politics and values, like work and decision making.

But here's the point I'd like to make: We don't want to talk

29

about these things in theory, we want to talk about them as they're practiced.

One reason we developed a family legal system, an economy, and traditions was that they would cause us to talk together about things that we were doing—things that had relevance in the real world.

—Linda

WHY #3: *The three steps will give your children a sense of values, consistency, and security in a time when all three are getting harder and harder to find.*

Because of the deteriorating values and confused morality prevalent in our society, children need more than ever before to be able to depend on their family to be reliable, predictable, and secure.

And in a world where we as adults often feel so frustrated, so swallowed up by bureaucratic and competitive pressures and societal problems beyond our control, *we* need, more than ever before, to be able to concentrate and focus on something we *can* influence—our family, our own children.

A family with simple laws, shared responsibility, and uniting traditions can offer children something known in a world of unknowns, something dependable in a world impossible to predict, a warm place in a world turned cold. Like an air supply, a stable family can make it possible for a child to explore new and unfamiliar environments, an opportunity to develop self-esteem and build character.

I've had some times when I've been with my friends and felt a little bad for some of them in a way that made me glad for some things we do. Like once when a kid was bragging that he could stay out as late as he wanted and his parents didn't care—well, I was glad mine did. It sounds funny but I felt glad for some rules because it meant they cared about me. Or when friends ask their parents for money whenever they need it—it's nice in a way but I usually have my own money that I've earned and it gives me a confident feeling.

—Talmadge, 14

Our last book, *Teaching Your Children Values,* provided a long "menu" of methods parents could use to teach their children values such as honesty, self-reliance, dependability, respect, discipline, and individuality. Many readers now tell us that the methods they like best (and that work best) are those that involve activities—family "exercises" that give examples or show the values in action. Stories or games or even "preaching" to kids may help them *understand* honesty or dependability or loyalty, but it's when they learn by *doing*—by repenting for breaking a law, by working and earning and owning things, and by participating in service- or ethics-oriented activities—that children really internalize the values we want to teach them.

As we travel, speak, or sign books in bookstores, readers of *Teaching Your Children Values* say, "In the book you talk about a set of family laws that teach justice and decision making and respect, but we need an outline of exactly what the laws are and how they work." Or, "You mention some family habits or patterns that encourage sexual abstinence, or peer-group courage, or a more peaceful atmosphere in the home, but how do you actually establish these traditions and get them going in a family?"

—Richard

This book is about these specifics, and about implementing some basic, recurring patterns in your family that will help you teach your children values.

The bottom-line reason for the three steps is that they increase children's chances to feel secure and be independent—in short to be *happy*. And regardless of the differences that exist between parents, the thing that unites us all is that we want our children to be happy.

Three "Don'ts"

Before we launch into the *how-tos*, we'd like to share some *don't*s with you. Based on our experiences, as well as on the feedback of others who have tried the three steps, we offer these little cautions, things to be careful of, three *don't*s to keep in mind as you start the program.

DON'T #1: *Don't try to do it all—or have it all—at once.*

Separate the three steps. Work on the legal system first. Family laws will create an improved sense of order and attention that will make it possible for you to teach other things. Getting your family rules working reasonably well will take from one to three months.

Next, establish your economy. Kids who are working, earning, saving, and buying on their own will take some of the pressure off of you and help prepare you to really enjoy the traditions of Step Three. Depending on how many children you have, how old they are, and your schedule, you may be able to get at least the fundamentals of your family economy established in a month or two—or it may take most of a year.

Only when the first two steps are functioning smoothly should you begin to build the traditions that will enhance your family's values and unity. Don't try to do too many too soon. At first build on the good traditions you already have. Then choose and develop additional traditions that work for *you* and that teach the principles or values that are important to you.

Keep in mind that just as you can't do it all at once, you can't *have* it all at once.

I was flipping through the TV channels one night in a hotel room and chanced on an interview with a leading feminist from the seventies and eighties who was, at age forty-three, pregnant with her first child and taking some time off to have and take care of her baby.

The interviewer, a somewhat irritating young man who was trying to promote controversy, said, "I'm going to read you a quote from someone—see if you can tell me who said this: 'Any woman with any brains or any guts deserves to do something more important than staying at home with little kids.' Do you know who said that?"

Of course she had said it. For a moment she was taken aback. But she regained her composure, looked the interviewer square in the face, and said, "I said it. And thank God I woke up before it was too late."

Then she went on: "Listen to me, young man—don't think I've given up anything. I still want to have it all. . . . I've just come to realize that you don't have to have it all at the same

time. What I want right now . . . what I need right now . . . is
to be with my child."

—Linda

We don't have our children in our home for very long—
just for one relatively short season of our lives. So it does
make sense, even if it requires some sacrifice and some
reprioritizing, even if we can't do it all at once, to take the
time to be with our children, to give them what they need,
to establish the three steps that can make our family feel
stronger and last longer.

Don't #2: *Don't try to follow every idea or suggestion
exactly—adapt things to fit your needs and style and your
own insights and ideas about your children.*

This book's suggestions are intentionally quite specific in
order to give you a clear idea of how they can work. But
you should think of them more as guidelines and as *examples* of how certain ideas might be implemented.
Change them to make them work within your circumstances. Think of them as a road map with options rather
than as a tunnel you have to go through blindly.

I have a wise old friend to whom I occasionally go for advice.
The reason I go (other than that he is a wise old friend) is that
he actually gives me specific advice. Instead of offering general platitudes or asking me if I've considered this option or
that, he listens to me and then tells me point-blank and specifically what he thinks I should do. I don't always do it, in
fact sometimes I think of an idea that I know is better for me
even as he is advising me to do something else.

The point is that specific advice helps you decide what to do. A lot of people won't give specific advice. They'll say, "You might consider this . . . ," or "Have you thought about that . . . ?" or "Well, I don't know, what do you think?"

Specific ideas cause action. Even when you don't completely accept them, they often make you think of something better.

—Richard

Read this book critically. Read with the intent of improving and "tailoring" our methods as well as of implementing them. Take our ideas and remodel them into yours.

No two families are alike. Our research for this book included input from families in our HOMEBASE organization—which includes two-parent, single-parent, blended, and step families; with parents who've been divorced or separated; with joint or primary custody. But *no* other family is exactly like yours. You have the responsibility as a parent to decide what is best for your family and your children.

DON'T #3: *Don't expect perfection or instant results.*

Improving an institution, changing a family, building abilities, values, character . . . these things don't happen overnight.

Think of yourself as a gardener planting seeds, watering, coaxing tiny plants out of the ground. Be patient. Work at it. Be satisfied with small progress and with periodic *moments* of joy when the results show.

35

We had been trying too hard to get our five-year-old, Eli, to quit teasing and badgering his little two-year-old sister, Charity. We had made "keeping the peace" one of our family laws. We'd told him how much she needed him to help her and to set an example. We'd tried to get her to quit screaming every time he looked at her sideways.

But he had perfected the art of teasing—taking great delight in it, becoming subtly and deviously adept at it. And she perfected her piercing, nerve-shattering scream of response.

One day at the grocery store I carried bags to the car with the two of them following me across the icy parking lot. I looked back to see Eli with his arm around Charity carefully helping her negotiate her way around the slick spots. Unmoved, I waited for him to find a snow bank and push her in. But he kept coming, patiently guiding her until he came right up to the car, looked up at my amazement with his arm still around her, and said (through his toothless grin), "Don't you wish you had a camera?"

—Linda

Moments. These moments of joy when the results of your hard work show are what we wait for. Be patient. Be as consistent as you can. Be gentle with yourself and realize that there will be times when you won't do as much or as well as you should. Keep trying and wait for the moments. Let the moments nourish you and motivate you as you work *gradually* on the big challenges and on overcoming the things that drive you crazy.

One of the things that drove me crazy for years, and that I still struggle with, is how fast the physical things in a home get broken, dirty, messy. It's a full-time job just taking care of the household, let alone the children. It's frustrating when you want to work at parenting but you have to spend your time at home on cleaning and cooking.

I remember one stage when I was totally frustrated by the physical condition of our house. Every drawer I opened held a combination of junk and treasures—all totally unrelated to one another. Five coats fell out of the hall closet each time it was opened. The curtain rod downstairs was broken and the new drapes were torn by children whose philosophy for anything that's stuck is "use force." Two quarts of the dread red Kool-Aid had been spilled on our nice light-beige wool carpet, and one of the couches was so beat up that the kids were literally falling in and scraping their arms on the springs.

The children had managed to run the electrical bill up to astronomical heights even though most of the light bulbs were burned out. A great, gaping flap of wallpaper hung limply on the wall of the laundry room where one of the boys had tried to build a tunnel for one of his trucks. We were tripping over the linoleum in several places in the kitchen where the seams were buckling due to the gallons of milk, juice, and punch that had been spilled over the years.

All the children were due to have their teeth checked and cleaned, which always ignited a rash of dental appointments to "fill the holes." Two children had teeth shooting out in every direction. One of them was being called Big Teeth by the bullies at school—so orthodontics was on my mind. I was a year behind on the baby's vaccinations, and the puppy needed shots. Another child was telling me that he couldn't see the blackboard from his desk at school.

The food situation was pretty bleak as well. After priding myself on making something different for dinner every night for the first few years of our marriage, I was now beginning to wonder how long the body can survive on macaroni and cheese before it starts looking a little orange.

Finally I decided it was time to pull myself up by the suspenders and do something about it. I remembered the principle we had taught the children one summer when we were trying to build a log cabin in the Oregon wilderness without the aid of any modern conveniences. We just tried to accomplish a little every day and we adopted the motto "You can eat an elephant if you just take one bite at a time."

I began picking one small thing in the house to take care of each day—and I congratulated myself on every small bit of progress.

Later, when we got serious about having a family legal system, economy, and traditions, I used the same method— "one bite at a time"—depending on patience and commitment to the long haul to help us reach our eventual goals.

—Linda

Now, with the *whys* and the *don't*s taken care of, let's move on to the most important question: *how?*

How is what this book is really all about. How to do it—step by step. How to set up family laws, a family economy, and family traditions that will bring your family together—and keep them together.

Let's get started.

1

Laying the Foundation: A Family Legal System

Anarchy exists in a country or state without laws. The word conjures visions of confusion, rebellion, danger— not unlike what we often see and feel in our families.

Legal systems not only protect our rights, our property, and our persons, they give us a stable, secure environment in which we can function and flourish. Ironically our limits give us freedom, whereas anarchy is the absence of both limits and freedom.

Children come into the world and into our families

needing and looking for limits and the security they give. When children are not given limits by their parents, they "push the envelope" farther and farther out looking for boundaries that can give their life some meaning.

Balancing Freedom and Limits

The "permissive parenting" of the seventies and eighties got lots of families into lots of trouble—and produced an unfortunately large number of insecure and confused children.

A good principle carried too far and not balanced by any counterweight becomes a bad principle. Children need freedom, options, and independence in order to grow and find their true selves. But the *balancing* principle is that children also need limits and order to feel secure and loved and to have a foundation on which to discover and build their own unique natures.

It is not difficult to reconcile these two principles or to see how they complement and benefit each other.

We have an interesting friend who lives in a rural area and loves to raise dogs. Year after year, regardless of their size or breed, the puppies he rears and sells or gives away are loving and good-tempered and yet seem to have remarkably unique personalities and characters. When asked what his secret is, he says, "Freedom and limits." Part of what he means is that he has a very large and interesting yard with a very high and secure fence. The puppies have room to roam and to learn, but they don't get out or get lost.

It's obvious that dogs in a tiny and confining fence or dogs with no fence at all wouldn't turn out nearly as well.

—Richard

Most parents who lose their children—really lose them to extreme rebellion, bitter alienation, or serious socially deviant behavior, either have a tight, cruel, arbitrary "fence" or no "fence" at all. Kids with no limits continually push toward more bizarre behavior, trying to find limits that would show their parents' concern and love. Kids given unrealistically strict and unbending rules won't be able to find their independence without rebellion.

In Pursuit of the Ideal Family

Most parents, when they try to imagine the ideal, think of an orderly family environment in which there is discipline, a schedule, respect, and even predictability. But families, almost by definition, seem to produce chaos, making the "orderly" notion seem like an unrealistic dream (or maybe an old movie).

When we started our family, I had some idyllic ideas. Replacing the restless, shiftless single life would be purpose, teamwork, and organization. Somewhere in my subconscious were things I wanted: the military efficiency and shared responsibility of the Trapp family in *The Sound of Music*, the calmness of Ozzie and Harriet or Ward and June Cleaver, even the words of a church song—"Roses bloom beneath our feet, all the earth's a garden sweet, making life a bliss complete, when there's love at home."

41

I also imagined that it would be easy to avoid the kinds of negative family behavior and discord that I'd seen and captured as bad examples in my mind: parents swearing, answering their children's questions with "Because I said so"; siblings bickering, arguing, fighting; and one particular mother I'd seen at the mall, dragging along two small boys. When one boy poked the other, she smacked him across the side of the head and yelled, "I'll teach you to hit your brother!"

—Richard

Reality sets in too fast, especially with both parents working, or going to school, or both. Single parents try to do everything. Being too busy, and too tired, we wonder how much we really like our own kids, while feeling guilty that we enjoy being at work more than we do being with them. We catch ourselves saying the very things we said we'd never say. Reality sets in.

As we get into real parenting, we all feel the need for something simple, workable, and practical, for something that can save us time rather than make us busier, for a way of setting limits and of teaching children the right kind of obedience.

The Objectives

So, with a dual awareness of the importance and value of a family legal system and of the difficulty of making one work, let's clarify and diagram exactly what we're talking about.

The goal is first to establish clear, simple *family laws* that children understand (and know the reasons for), laws that

1. Family Laws

OBJECTIVES:
safety
calmness
time management
priorities and choices
more orderly household

2. Consequences   3. Decision Making
(rewards and penalties)

make family members safer, calmer, and happier and that teach children the principle of obedience to law more than obedience to people.

Next we connect those laws to the concept of consequences—consistent *rewards and penalties*—while allowing for "repentance," through which amends can be made and a penalty or punishment avoided.

Finally we teach our children that some of life's big *decisions* are easy because they simply involve obedience to the laws and can be made quickly, even in advance. And we show them how other decisions involve multiple options instead of laws and thus require a different, more analytical kind of decision making.

Over time the implementation of a family legal system helps create order and peace in a home, *thoughtful* obedience in children, and some basic skills in the areas of time management, priorities, and choice making.

1. *Family Laws*

I remember so clearly our first attempt to set up some family laws. We were trying to start early—with two little daughters ages four and three. We sat down to have a "democratic meeting." Nominations were in order for family laws. "Don't hit little other girls," said the four-year-old. "Don't pud in puds," said the three-year-old, meaning "Don't plug in plugs," which came from my safety warnings. Before we were through, we had twenty-five laws, written upon a big chart in the exact words they were expressed.

It was a fun meeting, and that chart has become a family treasure, but no one remembered any of the laws, and they certainly didn't affect anyone's behavior.

—Richard

Looking back, we made some obvious mistakes in that first attempt. First of all, families are not democracies. In fact the whole idea of equality and "sameness" between parents and kids is one of the things that led to the permissive parenting that did so much damage to families. Parents are in charge of their children. They are responsible for their children, they are stewards of their children. Children *need* guidelines and limits from parents. It is fine for them to have input into those limits and to receive explanations regarding them, but not as part of a democratic "one man, one vote" process. Children will one day become parents and be responsible for their own children, but for now they are part of *your* family, which should be a place of listening and caring and explanation, but which must be more of a "benevolent dictatorship" or a "compassionate kingdom" than a democracy.

Still the *process* of involving children in thinking about rules and laws is a tremendously valuable and important one, as illustrated by the recollections of our oldest daughter.

I remember making up family laws as a four year old. I remember mom and dad sitting down with Shawni and me and explaining the ideas of laws and then asking us to make up the laws. We thought of some great stuff—from "Never hit little girls" to "Don't ruin things that aren't for ruining." Mom and dad wrote down all the laws we thought of and Shawni and I chose to color the whole paper green with crayons. The list was framed and posted. I liked that green framed list. Those were our own laws, not just mom and dad's laws.

I remember going through those laws and talking together about what should be the logical and functional punishment for breaking each law, and then later, deciding together to sort all these laws into five basic, more memorable laws. These were our family laws. Together we made them up, together we tried to keep them. It's so much more pleasant to keep your own laws than it is to keep someone else's laws.

Hey, I can't say I always kept those laws. But I believed in them, and I liked them, and they became principles to me, not just rules that must be kept in order to avoid punishment. I still keep those laws.

—Saren, 23

You can tell from reading this how much more effective this "consultation" process for developing laws was than if we had just imposed a set of rules. These are laws our daughters came up with on their own. In most cases they already accepted and were committed to them.

As Saren points out, we started out with too many, too complicated laws. Small children probably can't remember or stay conscious of more than five or six laws, even if they are very basic.

We ended up with five one-word laws:

1. *PEACE:* Defined in two simple ways:
   a. Don't fight . . . with hands or with words, with hitting or with arguing
   b. Don't lose your temper or yell
2. *ASKING:* Don't go somewhere or do something outside the normal schedule without asking and getting permission.
3. *ORDER:* Take care of your things, put away your clothes, and don't leave messes for others to clean up. Also, *do* things in the right *order*. Make your bed and brush your teeth before you leave for school. Do homework before you watch TV. Get in bed by bedtime. Be in by your curfew.
4. *RESPECT:* Be polite, particularly to your parents. Also, respect other people's rights, views, and property and respect the environment.
5. *OBEDIENCE:* Mind your parents. You may ask why and they will try to tell you, but then do it.

Keep in mind that with family laws you don't expect perfection—you set them up as guidelines and work at them gradually, doing better and better as time goes on. These five laws look like a wish list, obviously easier said than done, but it is a starting point—a *simple* starting point that kids can understand.

The best way to introduce the five laws is as part of a

major family discussion (*not* a "democratic election"). How you discuss the laws will depend on your children's ages, but the best way to start is by asking your children a series of questions designed to get them involved in the discussion. The *essential* questions are:

- *What are laws?* Talk about laws of nature, laws of the land, laws of a school, and so on—give a few examples of each.
- *What generally happens when people break laws?* Someone gets hurt or taken advantage of. *What about when people keep laws?* They're happier, safer, live together better.
- *What are some laws that would make our family safer, happier, calmer, better organized, fairer?* As ideas come up and are discussed, you will be able to distill them down to the five one-word laws. "*ORDER*" will be a catch-all for several things—from brushing teeth to curfews.
- *In what ways will each law prevent problems or make people happier?* Discuss the difficulties, extra work, hurt feelings, or worry that breaking each law can cause as well as the benefits of keeping each law.
- *Should we have penalties or punishments for breaking family laws . . . and rewards for keeping them?* Let some ideas and feelings come out, but suggest that you all think about it for a week or two while trying to live the laws, then meet again to talk about rewards and punishments.

Write the five laws on a big chart and just see what happens for a couple of weeks. Not much will change, but both you and the kids will notice which laws are followed, which aren't, and whether it makes a difference.

Talk about the laws whenever the opportunity arises, always reminding the children that they are still in the discussion stages of the process and that there will be another meeting to talk about *consequences, rewards,* and *penalties.*

Our family has a lot of family meetings on our laws and it gets really boring sometimes because we have them so often.

After I think back on each meeting, though, they all helped a little and we are getting better on our laws. I am happy to be able to go to these meetings because a lot of people don't have laws and I think that they help a lot. We are trying to work on them and make them better.

In every single meeting we have, my parents tell us that the reason we have these laws is because they can help us in our everyday lives and that if we didn't love you we wouldn't have laws and wouldn't care what you did and we would just let you do whatever you want.

—Noah, 12

We heard a touching story about a single mother in difficult circumstances who made a rather gallant effort to get our earlier book, *Teaching Your Children Values,* and apply it. She was out of work and on welfare and had only a twenty-dollar food certificate. She went to the market, bought a lemon, and with her change bought the book. Then she went home, sat on her bed with her three children, read aloud the part about family laws, and asked the kids if they would help her if she tried harder to be a better mom. The kids felt more trusted and more loved and said they would try. In that family the discussion process alone was the beginning of a new start.

—Linda

2. Consequences (rewards and penalties)

Your family laws won't make much difference or change much behavior until your children make a clear connection between their actions and the consequences.

The best consequence is a reward, and praise, recognition, and attention are the best rewards. These should be given as freely and profusely as possible as your children remember and keep the laws.

The best punishment or penalty is withholding rewards. The most appropriate penalties are natural (and therefore easily accepted *and* remembered) consequences of the laws that are broken. Spankings or corporal punishments of any kind don't work very well and teach the wrong thing (remember the lady who smacked her son and yelled, "I'll teach you to hit your brother").

The simplest penalties usually involve restitution. A child who makes a mess should clean it up. A child who hits should apologize. A child who goes somewhere without asking shouldn't get to go the next time. A child who speaks disrespectfully should have to repeat the conversation from the beginning, in a more respectful fashion.

The best way to *establish* these consequences is through another family meeting. Make a big deal out of it—perhaps meet over a special meal or in a special place. Start the discussion with these questions:

- *What are the consequences of breaking nature's laws or the government's laws?* If you defy the law of gravity, you'll fall. If you speed or run a stoplight, you may cause an accident or get a ticket.
- *What are the consequences of breaking our new family laws?*

Point out that fair laws have penalties for those who break them, not for those who don't. Right now if you forget to ask, your parents are punished—by having to worry about you. If you don't keep your things in order, someone else has to, and so on.

- *Is it best to have a reward for doing something right or a punishment for doing something wrong?* Both! Because that's how it works in real life—and in our family.
- *What do you think should be the reward and the punishment for each of our five family laws?* Kids may suggest all kinds of outlandish penalties. Guide the discussion along the lines of *natural* consequences—and toward the following suggestions:

PEACE: When two children are fighting (with actions or words), they must go to the "repenting place" (this can be any hard bench, or two hard chairs set next to each other, or a particular step on a staircase) and stay there until they can tell what *they* did wrong (not what the other child did—what *they* did, because it takes two to tangle, and both are almost always at fault in some way). Once they have explained what they've done wrong (to a parent or caregiver), they can apologize to the other child for that specific act, give him (or her) a hug, promise to try not to do it again, and leave.

What times we've had with our repenting bench! We've had children, wanting to get off the bench but unable to think of any way in which they were at fault, politely ask the other kid (whom they were furious at a moment before) what it was that they did wrong so that they could confess it and go. We've had kids with blood running down their face forgive a sibling who said, "Will you forgive me, I'll try not to do it again." We've had violent fights turn into more controlled "debates" by strong-willed children who would rather keep "discussing" than admit they did anything wrong.

Mainly, though, we've been relieved from the impossible role parents try to play—of being the judge and jury, figuring out who's right and who's wrong, doling out punishments and having the whole thing start over again two minutes later.

The bench became so important to us that once when we moved and had to furnish a new home, the very first thing we looked for and bought was a hard, uncomfortable bench.

—Linda

When we fit we need to go to wut we call the repnting bechk.

We have to say sory, we will try vary hard to not do it agen and will you fogiv me. I no falowing the laws is cool and this is 1 of them.

—*Charity, 7*

When one child breaks the law of *PEACE*, not by fighting with a sibling but by losing his temper, he goes to the "calm couch" for a time-out. He has to sit there until he can calm down and stop violating the peace. Again, the calm couch can be nearly any spot or piece of furniture, but it should be in a different, more physically comfortable place than the repenting bench.

ASKING: When a child goes somewhere without asking, without permission, without you knowing where he is, the penalty should be that the next time he wants to go somewhere, the answer is no. Make sure that you carefully explain to your children that this law is for their safety as well as for *your* peace of mind.

51

It was a warm and inviting night during my seventh grade year in Junior High. My friends and I were having a great time wandering aimlessly around neighborhoods and talking about anything and everything. The night slipped away quickly and before I knew it 12:00 o'clock rolled around which was and is my curfew. It was hard to ignore that it was so late but I wanted to stay there and talk until everyone was gone.

At about 12:30 the urge to go home (or the fear of not calling) was so strong it had to be done. I dialed the number slowly and with a deep down hope that my mother would answer, being that she is more calm than my dad. Of course with my luck it was my dad and he sounded furious although he said he was just worried—we know what this means (certain death). He came in the big yellow station wagon and didn't say a word till we got home, this was not a good sign. He began the usual lecture but this time he told me some of the reasons and I understood him better than I ever had. He explained why we have rules (the usual), but then said something I'd never thought of before: "rules give us freedom." This was new to me and needed to be thought about more before I could make a generic seventh grade rebuttal. This was a tough one. It made more sense to me after being explained wearing your seat belt restricts you in some ways but it can give you freedom by saving your life. The same thing comes with a curfew. Dangerous things happen after midnight (more than usual) and if you have this rule to come home at a certain time then you can have the freedom of being more trusted and have a better relationship with your parents. This gave me a broader perspective on everything and improved my communication with my dad.

—Jonah, 16

ORDER: Again, in keeping with the idea of connecting simple, clear consequences to behavior, the penalty for making a mess is to clean it up. The penalty for a messy room is to straighten it up before you can do anything else. When a mess-leaver isn't around and the cleanup has to be done by someone else (the parent), the child "owes you one" and has to clean something else to make it up. The child also "owes you one" if he fails to do things in the proper order or *sequence.* If he goes to school before making his bed and you have to make it for him, he should make your bed the next day. If he watches TV before his homework is done, he should not be able to watch the next day, even after he finishes his homework. If he misses his curfew, he can't go out the next time, and so on.

Like every other parent I've known, we wanted our children to be tidy—only we went to extremes—we tried everything. We had a system where if you left something out and someone else put it away, you owed him a quarter. For a while, if you found someone else's stuff out, you threw it on their bed, so they had to put it away before they could sleep. We invented a "gunny bag" (a laundry bag with painted-on eyes and nose and a drawstring mouth) who lived in the attic and came down and ate toys or clothes that were left out. We even remodeled and reorganized our house so that the kids' clothes were stored in the laundry room so that there weren't any clothes in their bedrooms to get thrown around and stepped on.

All of the ideas worked a little bit for a little while, but the old family law, of course, is the constant. Over time it has done the most good.

—Richard

Sometimes the law of *ORDER* needs to be supplemented —with examples, some help, and some extra recognition. One of Saren's memories illustrates this:

I remember one day—I must have been about nine years old—when we had a big family talk about order. Things were always messy and I think mom was ready to give up on us. Anyway, I remember dad having a big talk with us about pride and about the joy we feel when we work hard and can feel proud of a nice clean room. Then he did something that seemed really strange—he invited us into his room to watch him clean it. He kept saying things like "Oooh—I feel so good when this closet is organized," or "Mmmm, I'm proud of that sock drawer." When he was done, he put a sign on his door that said "pride." Somehow the concept really sunk in. All the nagging and "You have to clean your room before you can go play" hadn't made us want to change, so we'd kept our messy ways. But when I grasped the idea, the vision of my own room, my own things all neat and ordered, I wanted to see it actually happen. I wanted to earn a "PRIDE" sign for my bedroom door. I wanted people to be able to walk in and say, "Wow, what a nice room this is!"

Anyway, following the meeting, Shawni and I decided to go for the pride sign. We cleaned for what seemed like hours and hours, we sorted things out, we even cleaned out under our beds. We were doing something. When we got done and when we gave mom and dad a little tour, what a sense of accomplishment that was! They commented on how nice each aspect of the room looked—they let us show them under the beds, they rejoiced in our shelves of lined-up toys, they even marveled over our bed-making attempts (although I'm sure lumped up blankets showed through our bedspreads).

We felt pride. We got a sign on our door. I don't think our room was ever a total mess again. It was ours and it was clean.

—Saren, 23

RESPECT: When kids are rude or obnoxious, when they are disrespectful (to you, to others, to institutions, or to the environment), we've found that it's best to have them "start over." When disrespect occurs, a parent should say, "Hold it. Let's start over." If the disrespect was in response to a question you asked, say, "Let me ask you again, and you start over." This time ask with more respect *for your child* (say "please"), and let him have a second chance to answer with respect. Start over as many times as it takes to get it right. Also, "start over" if a child disrespects the environment by littering or if he speaks rudely to someone else or uses crude or unacceptable language.

When I have to do something over again ("start over") it's like if you were doing something else or you are mad and talking mean you would have to do it again.

When I have to do something over I feel mad and sort of discoraged and furious. Like one time after we did it over and over again and I got really, really furios so I got in major trouble.

But I think that having to do it over again is good so you don't get in trouble the first time. It's like you get another chance and you might get out of a bad habit. And when you do it over and over but you finally get it right you feel better— and everyone feels happier.

Also if I threw something on the floor or littered I'd be

55

almost sure to have someone in my family say, "Eli, start over!"

—Eli, 10

The "respect problem" has truly reached epidemic proportions in this country. Hearing a child speak to an adult, particularly a parent, in respectful terms is so rare that we're often quite surprised when we hear it.

So often parents ask me how they can get their children to treat them with respect. My first impulse is to say, "When you find out, let me know." We all have moments when our children shout back or issue demands. Part of the problem is just bad habits.

My mind turns back to several years when we had just arrived in England. Joyce, an outspoken young girl who was helping me one day, couldn't help overhearing a conversation between me and my oldest daughter, Saren (who was six). It was quite a heated conversation. After it was over and Saren had disappeared, Joyce said to me, "Why do you let Saren talk to you like that?"

"Like what?" I asked, completely amazed that she would think it was peculiar.

"Like she did this afternoon when you were 'having words' with her. Americans seem to let their children speak to them in such a dreadful manner!"

I was shocked, but I've always been grateful to that young lady for that question because it may have taken me quite some time to realize that Saren really did have a nasty tone in her voice. Having heard it quite often, my ears had become deaf. But in thinking about it, I decided that Joyce was absolutely right and that things were going to change! "It's all right to ask questions," I told Saren that evening, "but you must remember a certain tone of voice."

Still, when children get too near the line, I stop and say, "Are you yelling at me?" or "The way you said that makes me feel like you hate me. Is that true?"

The same principle applies with obedience. We parents get so used to giving orders that we don't really expect to be carried out that children stop hearing us, and we don't even notice whether they're obeyed. Children are very perceptive and know exactly what their parents expect of them. A great soul-searching family conference on the subject is highly recommended. It may change lots of bad habits that you hardly realized were there.

—Linda

OBEDIENCE: Your goal should not be blind "because I said so" obedience, but your children should know that as their parent you need (and intend) to be minded.

Make three commitments to children: (a) *that you'll think before you ask them to do something;* (b) *that you'll ask them politely;* and (c) *that you'll try to explain why if they ask.* In return ask them for their commitment to mind you. (Remind them again of the basic *difference* between parents and children—and that they will be parents someday and will expect *their* children to obey *them.*)

When your children disobey, start over again, this time emphasizing the trigger word of *please* in your request, which is their cue to say "Okay." or "Yes, Mom," and do it. If there is still disobedience or real defiance, the child should be sent to his or her room to think it over. After a little time for "simmering down" you should go in to talk to the child. You should both make some recommitments

57

to each other—that you will ask thoughtfully and with respect and that he will obey with respect. If the disobedience occurs away from home, repeat the "starting over" process until it works. Don't discipline a child in public. Talk about the problem when you get home.

I'm glad my parents (usually) recognized the differences between their children and disciplined us somewhat according to our personalities and emotional makeup. I have one brother who was always pushing the limits. I remember a couple of times when, as a small boy, he did something totally and openly rebellious and dad got extremely firm with him, sent him to his room, lectured him, set him straight at least forcefully, maybe angrily. The interesting thing is that I remember that afterward my brother actually felt better—he was cleansed by that punishment and really a little relieved that mom and dad really meant what they said. I was so opposite from that. I was a sensitive little girl who felt crushed if my dad even looked *upset or disappointed in something I'd done. I remember feeling so bad, and so grateful when I'd get a chance to "start over." The last thing I ever needed (or got) was a strong punishment.*

—Shawni, 21

REPENTING AND FORGIVING

One key element in a just and effective family behavior system involves concepts whose names may sound too religious and too impractical to work in today's world. These include such old-fashioned ideas as forgiveness, apology, mercy, restitution, absolution, and *repentance*.

As parents we need to remember that the *purpose* of our family laws and rules is not to punish or to restrict or to exercise control, it is to *teach* and *learn* and *progress* and *improve* and *mature*. Children (and adults) grow the most when they correct *themselves,* when they learn from their mistakes, when they independently decide to improve or to do better.

Therefore it's critically important to give children every chance to correct themselves, to repent, to avoid their punishment by making restitution. And we must *always* give them the benefit of the doubt.

Authoritarian parents who are so strict, unbending, and rule-conscious that they take pride in meting out swift "justice" are in as great danger of losing their kids as parents who provide no discipline at all. Keep the following modifying principles or guidelines in mind:

- *Have rules but provide for exceptions.* A curfew is important, but be willing to modify it, for example, when a child calls before he should be home and tells you he's in the middle of watching a video and doesn't have a ride home until it's over.
- *Design your punishments or penalties so that children can avoid them by "repenting."* For example, the procedure for getting off of the "repenting bench" mentioned earlier.
- *Try to give children responsibility for choices, but never hold bad decisions over their heads—forgive them whenever they ask.*
- *Work hard at being the best parent you can be, but realize how far from perfect we all are and apologize to your kids*

when you make a mistake. This covers anything from blaming a child for something he didn't do to losing your temper. Say you're sorry and mean it!

Like so many parts of parenting, a system of rules or laws takes time to produce results—and sometimes you don't realize you've had much effect until children are far away and writing back. Here's another example:

It's interesting, from an ocean away, to think back on our family's "legal system." All of the rules finally jelled down to the five family laws: respect, peace, asking, order, and obedience. Each of these laws cover so much. They all had their own punishments. If we went somewhere without asking, we wouldn't be able to go next time we wanted to go somewhere. That was a hard punishment, so I usually kept the law of asking. If we fought with each other, we'd have to go to the repenting bench. I hated the repenting bench. It seemed like a waste of time to sit there with the person you were fighting with until we decided to repent. It didn't seem to cut down on the arguments. But it did end the fight we were having and allowed us to repent instead of getting punished. It was a good learning experience. I always felt better after I repented.

To help us remember the five family laws, dad made up a little song about them which I thought was rather silly. It did help us remember the laws, though. It had a catchy little tune. I always tried to obey the family laws, not just because I didn't want a punishment, but because I knew they were important. I really respected my parents and their knowledge. Mom was always stressing the importance of the laws. Peace was one of the hardest laws to obey, because I had a short temper. But through the family's help, I have overcome it. These five laws have worked very well in our family and I'm sure I'll use them when I have a family of my own. They definitely strengthen families.

—Josh, 19

3. Decision Making

The final element in a good family legal system is something that goes beyond laws. It is helping your children learn to make good decisions. If we can teach our children *how* to decide, *how* to choose right from wrong, *how* to select the best option, we will help them avoid not only the penalties of breaking the law, but the harsh consequences of wrong choices.

The easiest decisions in life are those that are governed by *laws*. In theory they are easy because the only real decision to be made is whether or not to keep the law. Whether the law is a red light, a family rule, or gravity, your decision is binary; you keep it or you break it, and usually the consequences are clear. Children (and adults) who understand this can save their analytical thought and effort for tougher decisions, those that have multiple options and those that involve making assumptions or speculating about the future.

It is important for small children to be able to differentiate between situations governed by laws and situations governed by decisions. The simplest way to teach this difference to preschoolers and early elementary age kids is with little "dialogue games." For example:

Parent: O.K. you know what laws are, right?

Child (prompted as necessary): Things that we should follow—and if we don't we will have a punishment or a problem.

Parent: Yes. Sometimes they are called values; sometimes they're called laws. There are two things you can do with a law. You can keep it or you can break it. If you keep a law you'll be happier. What are some laws you can think of?

Child (especially if you've just worked on the family laws suggested in this book): Well, there's *PEACE* and *ORDER.*

Parent: Right. These are our family laws. And there are punishments when we don't keep them, right?

Child: Unless we repent.

Parent: Exactly! And we're happier in our family if we keep those laws. Now are there any other kinds of laws? Do we have some laws in our town or in our country?

Child (promoted as necessary): Wear seat belts, don't drive too fast, don't take things that belong to other people.

Parent: And are there punishments if we break those laws?

Child: You could get hurt or you could get arrested.

Parent: Yes, that's right. You really do understand about laws! Does *nature* have any laws?

Child (prompted): The law of gravity, the law that when it's winter you'll be cold outside unless you wear a coat.

Parent: Any punishments for breaking these?

Child: You could fall down or you could freeze.

Parent Is there a law for everything?

Child (unsure)

Parent: Well, is there a law that tells us what color of shirt we have to wear or what movie to go to or what sport we have to like?

Child: No.

Parent: When there isn't a law what can we do?

Child: We can choose.

Parent: Right—we can choose—we can make a choice. Do you know another name for a choice?

Child (prompted): A *decision.*

Parent: Some decisions don't matter very much, like whether you have orange juice or apple juice at breakfast. But some decisions matter a lot. Can you think of some?

Child (prompted): If you eat healthy food or just eat candy. If you are nice to everyone or just to your friends. If you do your best at school or just fool around.

Parent: Do decisions make a difference?

Child (prompted): Yes. There are punishments or problems when we make bad decisions just like when we break laws.

There are two very important things that parents can do to help children improve their decision-making abilities while they are in grade school, things that will protect them and prepare them for the weighty and potentially dangerous choices they will have to make as adolescents and young adults:

1. *Let them start out making decisions about saving and spending money* when they are quite young. You can start

this process with your children as early as eight years old. They'll make mistakes *early*, when the consequences are minor—and learn the principles of self-reliance and delayed gratification while they are still very impressionable. *How* to give them the opportunities to make the decisions is the topic of Step Two of this book.

2. *Help them make a list of "decisions in advance."* Upper-grade school-age children (eight to eleven or so) are very conceptual and capable of handling "scenario thinking." Thus you can help prepare them for dangerous or difficult situations by helping them make decisions before they are actually involved in them.

Have your child (in some special place, perhaps in the back of a diary or journal) make a list of "decisions in advance" or "decisions I have already made."

Get them to start thinking about these decisions with a discussion something like the following:

"Son, right now you're only ten years old, but are there some decisions you can already make about what you will do or won't do when you're older? Think about when you're twelve, or fourteen, or sixteen—are there some things you can decide right now?"

With a little thinking and a few hints, some of the major issues they'll face will start to come up.

"I could decide right now never to do drugs."

Or, "I can decide always to try to be honest."

Or, "I can decide not to smoke."

Or, "I can decide to wear a seat belt . . . or tell friends I'm driving with not to drive too fast . . . or not to be in a car with a driver who's been drinking."

Don't try to finish the list in one day. Get it started in a first discussion and then approach it again in a week or two. Make some suggestions. Let your child think about them. Tell him some decisions *you've* made in advance. Tell him some you *wish* you'd made when you were his age. Give him a lot of praise for any good ideas he comes up with.

When you feel that the time is right, suggest that he write down the decisions he's made in advance—in some special place, such as his diary—and that he *sign* each item on the list, making it like a contract with himself or an official pledge. Offer to sign them yourself, too, as his "witness." (Some children are intrigued by an "official" witnessed document or contract. Anything you can to do help the child see that he or she is making a serious commitment is useful.) Explain that he can add to his list whenever he thinks of additional decisions that he can make in advance.

As children approach dating age, decisions in advance can be added about levels of physical intimacy and things they will not do with a member of the opposite sex.

There are two additional critical elements in this process. First, make sure your child understands the reason behind the decisions in advance—that the *best* and *strongest* time to make a decision is *before* you're faced with it—while you can think clearly. When we're in the middle of a situation and we feel pressure (or temptation), it is much easier to make the wrong choice. Second, help your child prepare for actually sticking to the decisions through scenarios or by role-playing for each decision he's made in advance. Use your imagination. If he says he's decided to never do drugs, say something like, "Okay, let's imagine you are fifteen years old and at a party. Three of your best friends are trying something you know is drugs. They seem to be enjoying it, it doesn't seem to be hurting them, and they really want you to try it too. They say that one time couldn't hurt you. They call you chicken. They tell you you'll never know how it feels unless you at least try it once. A girl you like comes over and asks what's wrong, why won't you try a little . . . and so on." This will help him understand just how hard it is to live up to decisions made in advance, but will also give him an added appreciation for the importance of the process.

I had an experience that illustrates the importance of "walking through" an advance decision. I was in a boat out on a lake fishing with a young man—not one of my own children but a boy I knew well and cared a lot about.

We were talking about dating (something he'd just become involved with), and he mentioned that he believed in sexual abstinence before marriage—and gave some great reasons for his feelings. I got the impression that he was sincere but didn't have much of a clue about how hard it would be or the situations he might find himself in.

So I described a situation for him—being with a girl he really liked, feeling an intense attraction, having her make some advances and some suggestions, feeling some pressure to do what others had bragged to him about. I described the scenario in detail and asked him what he would do.

He said, "I'd take her home."

I asked him to elaborate, to be as specific as I had been.

He said, a little embarrassed, "Okay, I'd sit up, I'd get my hands on the steering wheel, I'd turn the key and start the car. I'd say, 'I think it's time to go,' and so on."

A couple of years later that boy came up to me with a very serious look on his face. "It happened," he said.

"What happened?" I asked, not having any idea what he was talking about.

"It happened," he said, "you know—what you said in the boat."

"What did you do?"

He smiled. "I sat up, I got my hands on the steering wheel, I turned on the key and started the car. . . ."

Then his serious look came back. "I never realized how hard it could be. If I hadn't rehearsed it in my mind, I wouldn't have been able to stop."

—Richard

Have your son or daughter wait to sign any item on his or her list until you've walked through a couple of difficult scenarios together. Then, when you're both sure you understand how the decision applies to hard, real situations, he or she can sign.

My decisions were first written out on a sheet of paper at the age of eight along with typical spelling errors of an eight-year-old and a scribble of a signature following all decisions including "I will not take drugs," "I will find a good wife," "I will be nice to my kids," and "I will not smoke." (I think I meant drink or smoke.) These decisions were solid in my mind, in concrete, signed and everything.

I remember not thinking too long about them that first time because I wanted to get finished so I could go outside and go on a bike ride. Little did I know that these "decisions in advance" would be so important throughout my life.

My list of decisions was put away and pretty much forgotten about except for in the back of my mind they were still there. Years past and at the age of twelve these decisions in advance were again found and revised and a few were added, all beginning with the words "I will" or "I will not." And again they were all signed with my signature. I've worked on them and recommitted myself on them a few times since. I could never really forget them because I know where they are—on the back page of my big journal.

These decisions in advance took up so little time to make but made such a big difference. I'm old enough now to know. When an important decision needed to be made without hesitation the answer has been strong and one-sided with nothing or no one to change my mind. For example, there have been parties that were easy not to go to because I knew there would be drinking. Decisions in advance are powerful.

—Jonah, 16

Parents' Part

It goes without saying that the most effective way you can teach family laws is to live them yourself. At the same time children need to understand that while some of the family laws apply to both parents and children, other laws apply in a different way. PEACE and ORDER apply equally. You should be willing to go and sit on the repenting bench or the calm couch if your behavior merits it, and your room and your schedule ought to be as orderly as theirs.

While parents do not ask their children for permission, they should let children know where they are and when they will be back, and they should remember that *asking* a child to do something is more polite and more respectful than telling him or her (and more effective).

Children's respect for parents is shown, among other

things, by obedience. Parents' respect for children is shown by asking their opinions and helping them make their own decisions.

A discussion about how some family laws apply differently to parents is a good idea. Emphasize that parents are in charge of and responsible for their children—just as those children will one day be in charge of their own family and responsible for their own children.

There are three particular aspects of a family legal system that are usually very difficult for parents to observe—enough so that they deserve further discussion.

APOLOGIZING

How hard it is to admit to our kids that we've been wrong! But how much it does for communication and for trust! When you've made a mistake, or blamed the wrong child, or gotten angry when you shouldn't have, say you're sorry!

I remember years ago when one of our daughters came in well past her curfew. I jumped all over her, chewed her out, accused her of insensitivity and irresponsibility, and grounded her.

The next day I found out that the reason she was late was that a friend had hurt herself and our daughter was trying to help her. I went down to her room, intending to apologize.

I did get started. I said, "I'm sorry. I didn't know . . ." And then the old parental instincts kicked in: ". . . but have you ever heard of phones? Couldn't you at least have called so we wouldn't worry?"

Predictably, she met my renewed anger with sarcasm. "Oh,

sorry, Dad, I didn't know what I was thinking—I should have told her to just go bleed to death, I have to call my father."

It took me until the next night to try again. This time I swallowed the urge to be right and just said I was sorry. Her eyes misted up, as mine did, and as we hugged, she said, "It's okay, Dad, I can tell you're really trying."

—Richard

If you are a two-parent family, apologizing to each other is as important as apologizing to your children. Let them see you apologize and make amends with each other—with your spouse (their mother or father). Make it a rule: If they see you fight or disagree, be sure they also see you resolving and apologizing.

RESPECTING OUR CHILDREN

If one of the family laws is respect, let it work both ways. It is truly shocking how we sometimes speak to our children—worse than we would speak to anyone else—as though they were servants or objects or extreme irritations.

Imagine that your children were your best friends—or your best friends' children. Use courtesy. Ask rather than tell. Say please, thank you, and excuse me. Firmness and kindness are not opposites or mutually exclusive. Mutual respect generates calmness and cooperation.

I remember having something of an epiphany in the middle of the night once with one of our babies. This child was keeping us up all night. Linda was exhausted and I was trying to settle the baby down with his bottle. But he was restless and colicky and just would not stop crying. I had an early meeting the next morning and knew I needed sleep. I was becoming more and more angry at the howling one-year-old.

He finally calmed down for a minute and I looked out the window into the starlight and had a thought: Our roles could be reversed. I had come to earth thirty years before this son of mine. He could have come before me and he would be the one losing sleep, trying to quiet me down and getting angry. I could just as easily have been the colicky infant, helpless and uncomfortable, anxious for what soothing my parents could provide.

Our children are equal to us in every way. We should respect them as brothers and sisters. They deserve as much respect from us as we do from them.

—Richard

Practicing the Law of *PEACE*

Nothing makes a family work better than *calmness*. In an atmosphere of peace children become more cooperative and more loving. Hard as it is, try to stay calm. Talk your way through the day in advance. Tell yourself when you get up that you'll have irritations that day but you'll stay calm—like the eye of a hurricane.

I heard a story that made the point:

A man shopping in his neighborhood grocery store noticed a mother pushing a grocery cart with a howling two-year-old seated in the cart's infant seat. He became involved in the unfolding drama as he watched her walk down the aisle. He heard her say in a low, calm voice, "Now, Jessica, it's not so bad. We've just got a few more things to find and we'll be on our way." The weeping and wailing could be heard all over the store, and he noticed her again at the dairy case. She was placidly saying, "Jessica, it really isn't that painful. You can make it for just a few more minutes, can't you? We're almost finished!"

The man watched the mother go through the checkout stand with her child still sniffling and whining and couldn't resist the urge to speak to her on the way out.

"I just have to tell you," he said as the automatic doors flew open, "how impressed I am with the way you speak to your child." She looked confused for a moment and then smiled and said, "Oh, there's something you should know—I am Jessica!"

—Linda

First Intermission

One of the problems with writing family or parenting books is that people get the idea that things always go smoothly in *your* house—that *your* family laws work perfectly.

Perish the thought! Families are remarkably similar in that we all struggle. We all have ups and downs. And it always looks easier for other families than for us.

Let's spend this intermission commiserating with one another as parents—and realizing that parenting isn't a science made up of perfected formulas that always work the same way. The "legal system" just discussed will help your family as it has helped ours, but it's not a panacea and it won't work overnight.

The things that unite parents are that we all love our kids and we're all *trying* . . . and we all need a sense of humor. Let us mention a few examples that come to mind. They didn't seem as funny when they happened as they do now. In fact, have you noticed that (Crisis + Time = Humor) in families?

One day at a political convention where Richard was running for office, I left to go home a little early with six tired, hungry children following behind me like ducklings. Suddenly one of them accidentally (or maybe on purpose) stepped on another's foot, and a full-fledged yelling fight broke out.

Exhausted, hungry, grumpy, and laden with problems myself, I snapped out a nasty correction and tried to find out who did what to whom and who started what first and why. (After all, we were a long way from our repenting bench, and I was nowhere near calm enough to ask them politely to quietly consider what each had done wrong.)

Not far behind us two men whom I didn't recognize were closing in on us fast. I quickly tried to smooth things over, embarrassed by every child who had chimed in on the argument and not very happy with myself either.

The two men quickened their pace. "Well, if it isn't Linda Eyre!" one of them blurted out. "You just made my day," he chuckled as I stumbled over niceties amid still-growling children. "My wife will be thrilled to know that the Eyres fight too!"

I tried to laugh. I was embarrassed, but it was funny. I was red-faced, but most of all I was mortified that anyone would think that the Eyres didn't fight. Please know . . . it's a promise . . . WE FIGHT!

—Linda

All families try to put on their best face in public. Most of the family problems we see are our own—which sometimes gives us the false idea that our families are more disrespectful or have more sibling rivalries and more hassles than others. That's why it's almost refreshing and reassuring when we see other families having little fights or disagreements in public. It's evidence that we're not alone in our struggle.

Sometimes the embarrassing moments can really be public. Just as our book *Teaching Your Children Values* was hitting the best-seller lists, the book and our whole family was featured on "Oprah"! We taped the show in Chicago. When it was broadcast a few days later, we happened to be in Las Vegas for a basketball tournament that our son's team was playing in.

We watched ourselves on the show in our hotel room and then went downstairs to the buffet for lunch. The long waiting line wound through the slot machines, and our kids naturally asked me for quarters. I absentmindedly handed them the change from my pockets and they plopped it into the slots and pulled the handles.

Suddenly three middle-aged ladies came up to me with bright looks of excited recognition on their faces. "Hey—we just saw you all on 'Oprah'! You were talking about"—here they paused, looked embarrassed, glancing around at our children—"teaching children values." One of them quickly added, "Don't worry, we won't tell."

—Richard

The books and articles we read by "parenting experts" often depress us more than they help—because they make parenting seem so complex that we feel inadequate, or because the examples they give always seem to work out so much better than when we try the same things in our own families. Sometimes what we need is not another method or another technique or another example of how well something worked. What we need are examples of some frustrations or failures—just enough to reassure us that we're not the only ones who are struggling.

A few years ago I got so tired of unrealistic "here's how to do everything" parenting books that I wrote a book for frustrated mothers called *I Didn't Plan to Be a Witch*. It was an easy book to write. All I did was recall and write down my frustrations.

I really didn't plan to be a witch, but on occasion, as my children will attest, I can be.

That's not the only thing I didn't plan. I didn't plan to be ecstatic over a C-plus on the report card of our child with a left-brain learning disability. Nor did I plan on a child losing his backpack regularly or forgetting all about his social studies homework. (When his teacher calls to inform me of another episode of forgetfulness, I pray that she doesn't know that we also wrote a book called *Teaching Your Children Responsibility*.)

I didn't plan to have a high school sophomore who has a major crisis in her life almost every other day because she is totally overcommitted and likes it that way. If it isn't reading *David Copperfield* in one night, it is decorating the halls for "The Battle of the Classes."

I didn't plan to have a five-year-old who demands my total attention every waking moment—a need that intensifies in the grocery store or when I'm in a hurry or when I'm on the phone.

I didn't plan to produce two perfectionists who vent their frustrations about everything not being perfect (including the weird seeds in the bread) by yelling at me! And I certainly didn't plan to have a husband whose idea of a good time is flossing his teeth in bed.

I didn't plan to have a painfully shy child, or one who loses his temper at the drop of a hat, or one who has somehow become involved with the wrong kind of friends. I didn't plan any of it. Parents never do. The question usually isn't planning—it's coping!

—Linda

None of us planned to lose our tempers or to be knocked off balance by the problems we face. None of us planned to be a "witch," but all of us need help making sure it happens less frequently. What we need is a plan—not a quick fix, not a cure-all, not a panacea—but an overall strategy that will help us stay focused on the basics of what we want to accomplish in our families.

The family legal system we've developed, which concentrates on following basic rules and making good decisions, is a good first step in that strategy.

Remember, as you work on your own legal system, that you're looking for long-term results. The "payoffs" sometimes don't come until much later. One of our rewards came when our daughter Saren, who is helping children in an orphanage in Bulgaria, decided to sit down and write a foreword for this book. By the time we received her letter, we already had a foreword, so we've decided to include it as part of this "intermission." We think it makes a tremendous statement about the reasons to give children responsibility.

In case anyone wonders why Richard and Linda Eyre are qualified to put together a book on families, let me just tell you that I have the best, most outstanding family imaginable. And despite the fact that there have been many times in my life when I wouldn't admit this, my parents have done a superb job. Family has always come first for them, and their commitment led to the commitment of all us kids to each other and to our parents.

Through contact with families in school, college, and work, I've seen a bunch of messed up things. I've seen a lot of misery. Family can be the best thing in a person's life. It can also be the greatest source of pain and sorrow. The simple principles in this book are true and lasting constants. A person needs to be a functioning, contributing, partaking part of some institution in order to be happy. What better institution than the family! The family is where we all start out in life and whether we start out right or not is going to affect our whole life. This is serious stuff.

I've become grateful for the responsibility and discipline I learned in my family. I just want to thank my parents from the bottom of my heart. They've thought hard, they've worked hard, they've learned through trial and failure and I'm so glad they've taken the opportunity to share their wealth of experience with you.

—Saren, 23

As you can tell from our earlier examples, Saren's memories are probably a bit colored by the passage of time, and her comments are probably rendered a bit more glowing by the fact that "absence makes the heart grow fonder." Still, as you can imagine, her words mean a great deal to us. We like to think that her thoughts show that children who are given responsibility throughout their childhood are likely to develop a sense of appreciation for their parents' efforts—as well as valuable perspective on the importance of family life.

Now let's move on to the second step—building a family economy—which will lead to more sharing of family responsibilities—and thus to less-stressed parents and better-prepared children.

2

Paying Your Dues: A Family Economy

In our society we give our children *license* too early and *responsibility* too late. We give them privileges—to stay out, to date, to consume, to use, to be entertained, to experiment before they are capable or appreciative or mature or ready. Yet we do not give them responsibility for their possessions, their money, their jobs, their choices, or their behavior until they are too old and the consequences of their mistakes are too severe.

Actually by the time children are eight years old, they are capable of accepting responsibility for earning their own money, buying their own clothes, totally caring for their own room and their own things, systematized savings for their education, and sharing the general responsibility for the home.

Giving this kind of early responsibility does not rob children of their childhood—on the contrary, it gives them the appreciation, the perspective, and the beginnings of self-reliance and self-esteem that enhance childhood joys.

We have friends who were so determined to teach their young children responsibility that, at considerable inconvenience, they moved to the country and started a small farm. To some extent it worked. The children gathered eggs, milked a cow, planted and harvested vegetables, and saw the obvious benefits of their work and also the obvious consequences of forgetting or failing at a responsibility.

It was hard on the parents, though, who missed their urban home, lived farther away from their work, and found that it took considerable time to help children accept and fulfill responsibilities. But they did accomplish many of their goals. By setting up charts to mark off and by developing some financial rewards, they were able to motivate their kids to accept the farm responsibilities. They raised calves for sale, sold eggs and milk, and got a small percentage of the farm income.

Another similar family, impressed with the results of the first but unwilling to move to a farm, decided to try to duplicate the principles and ideas of giving responsibility with rewards—but in a suburban setting rather than on a farm. They divided household responsibilities, paid kids for sharing certain parts of the upkeep (other than their own rooms), set up a family bank that paid interest to motivate saving, and let children buy their own clothing and personal effects with the money they earned.

It took some time and effort by the parents of this second family to set up, monitor, and motivate the responsibility system (as it had with the farm family), but the results were equally good and equally worth the effort.

—Linda

There are as many responsibilities today as yesterday, as many in the city as in the country. But in earlier and more rural times the family economy provided more obvious opportunities for responsibility. Crops were planted, cultivated, harvested, and sold. Eggs were gathered, clothes were made, butter was churned, fields and animals were cared for, and the results were visible and the consequences clear. If cows were not milked, they let you know about it. If the fields weren't planted, there was no harvest. Money came in in proportion to how much work people did and how well they did it.

Today family economies are more subtle and more hidden. Most of what we need is bought rather than made or grown. Most of our jobs don't produce anything tangible that children can see. Even the work of caring for a house is less noticeable because of the efficiency of "modern conveniences."

Nevertheless our modern-day families still face responsibilities and needs, and parents *can* establish responsibility, so that their children become self-reliant, learn the discipline of delayed gratification, and have the opportunities to make good decisions.

One of my most vivid memories is the summer that dad and mom decided to take a rather drastic approach to teaching us responsibility. They had saved up vacation time and money and they took us high into the Blue Mountains of eastern Oregon to "live like the pioneers and build our own log cabin." I was 13. One of my jobs was to be the scribe and record all our experiences. Sometimes I drew pictures because it was hard to describe how dirty people get or how funny the cabin looked.

We did learn a lot. (Mostly we learned how much we missed things like plumbing and friends and home.) Experiences like that are always better when you look back on them—but it did teach us many things. But I really think that what we did at home, year in and year out with our jobs and our checkbooks and our family bank, taught us more about responsibility than our "crash course" in Oregon.

—Shawni, 21

Opportunities for Responsibility

In the last section we said that the absence of *laws* in a society produces *anarchy*. There is not quite as neat or simple a name for what happens to a society without a working economic system, but there are plenty of current examples in our world, particularly in the former communist countries now struggling to develop free market economies.

At present we have two daughters doing humanitarian service and missionary work in Eastern Europe—one in Romania and one in Bulgaria. In an effort to better understand the work they're doing, we exchanged a vacation we'd been waiting for and saving for a couple of years for three weeks of work as volunteers in an institution for handicapped orphans in the Transylvanian Alps of Romania.

What we learned there is material enough for another book, but we also observed a society struggling to find the order and motivation of a market economy in the wake of the devastating economic effects of communism. Economically things were topsy-turvy. We went to a full-fledged opera that cost five cents and bought Cokes at intermission that cost fifty cents. We met doctors, who earned seventy dollars a month, who were saving to buy TV sets that cost ten months' wages. One woman told us, "Under communism everyone had money, but there was nothing to buy. Now everything is for sale, but no one has any money."

Still, we saw the effects of a beginning economy. People told us they were working hard and long and with objectives for the first time because they could earn, could save, could better themselves, could determine their own destiny.

—Richard

An economy (as we use the word here) is a system whereby people can earn, save, and buy. But it is much more than that. It requires responsibility and discipline, and it provides motivation. It can help children develop confidence and a self-reliant self-image. It offers training for decision making, for delayed gratification, for prioritizing, and for caring for others.

The Objectives

The three elements of a family economy can be diagrammed:

1. Ways for Children to *Earn* Their Own Money

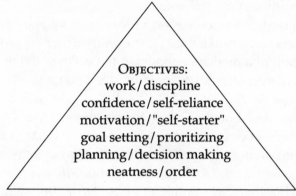

OBJECTIVES:
work/discipline
confidence/self-reliance
motivation/"self-starter"
goal setting/prioritizing
planning/decision making
neatness/order

2. Ways to *Save*, Invest,   3. Ways to *Spend* Money Wisely
   Earn Interest   and Perceive Ownership

It is interesting that most parents know and agree on the qualities or characteristics they would like to see develop in their children. We want confident, self-reliant kids who know how to work, who are motivated and can get themselves going. We want them to be able to set goals and have the right priorities, to be able to plan ahead and make good decisions, and to be orderly and take care of their things.

But these are not qualities or abilities that we can give our children or that they will acquire at a young age by chance or by luck. They must learn and develop them for themselves, and wise parents create an environment or a system *within* our families that promotes or *calls* for these characteristics.

Our family was very young when we began to realize how counterproductive modern society can be with regard to giving children some of the lessons they need. A couple of incidents led to our efforts to set up a family economy.

Seven-year-old Shawni needed a birthday present for a friend, so I had taken her to a toy store. She said she wanted a "big present," but everything she liked was expensive. I told her they cost too much and she said, "Well, Dad, why do you care, you can just write a number on one of those little checks." I realized that she had very little idea that things cost real money, that I'd had to work for the money, or that using checks or credit cards meant spending real money.

A few days later five-year-old Josh came home from kindergarten missing a shoe. I asked him where in the world his shoe was. He answered (very conversationally) that water was running down the ditch by the sidewalk. He'd been looking for a boat and tried his shoe. It went under a bridge and didn't come out.

I said a typical parent thing: "Do you know how much that shoe cost?" Josh stared back innocently and shook his head. I proceeded to lecture him about taking care of his things.

Trying to defend himself, Josh said something that shocked me. He said, "Well, it wasn't my shoe!"

"Whose was it?" I said, genuinely confused.

"It was yours," he replied.

For a minute I thought he'd floated one of my shoes down the ditch. But it was his little foot I was looking at in just a wet sock. He went on, "It was your shoe. You bought it. And you'll probably buy me another one."

Josh didn't perceive ownership. He was using a shoe I'd bought. And he didn't perceive much inconvenience in me buying another one.

Josh and Shawni were also in the habit of coming into our bedroom early each Saturday morning and demanding their allowance—money they felt they were entitled to and that bore no connection to any effort or performance on their part.

Both of the children had been to my office, which they liked a lot. There were gadgets and games there—copiers and computers. They didn't perceive that there was hard work going on there or money being made. The work, the earning, the spending, the saving, the ownership, and the care—and the connections between all of them, which are obvious on a farm—were invisible to my children. We started trying to think of ways to make them visible.

—Richard

The family economy system outlined here works best when it is introduced in simple form to five-, six-, and seven-year-olds and established in full force when the children turn eight. With some modifications it can also be effective with older children (as explained at the end of this section).

Let's go back to the objectives listed inside the triangular diagram. These qualities, which all parents want their children to develop, can be taught and practiced, facilitated and reinforced, by a simple family economy in which children have a way to: (a) learn discipline and work to *earn* money; (b) plan and set goals and *save* money; and (c) set priorities and make decisions in *spending* money.

1. Learning to Earn—The Peg System

An economy "starts" with earning money. When children earn money as a result of (and in proportion to) their

86

efforts, they perceive it (and the things they buy with it) as *theirs,* and thus begin to feel responsible.

There are three steps in setting up the "earning" part of the family economy—first a family discussion about the division of family responsibilities, then a "pegboard" or other recording system to help children keep track of their responsibilities, and finally a "payday" when they receive "earnings" that are proportionate to how well they performed their assignments.

SPLITTING UP FAMILY RESPONSIBILITIES

Children usually have little idea of how much *work* it takes to run a household. Often they do not have the added security and feelings of self-worth that come from doing their share and assuming part of the responsibility.

The first thing to do is to make a long list of "what it takes to run this house." Include everything—from "keeping the family room tidy and clean" (list every room separately), to preparing dinner (list every meal for every day separately), to washing and drying dishes, to mowing the lawn, to taking out the garbage, to doing the laundry. Also list things like buying food and earning the money to buy food.

With this long list as your visual aid, sit down and have a family discussion. Explain that there's a lot of work to do but that it all needs to be done, and show how it makes the family happier (pick out a few things on the list and ask what would happen if they didn't get done).

Count the number of things on the list and the total number of people in your family. Divide the former by the latter. Ask if that's the best way to divide up the work— with everyone doing the same percentage of the tasks. Talk about how some jobs take much longer than others— especially earning the money the family needs. If they're not already on the list, children will bring up going to school and doing homework. Put both on the list and talk about how education is an important part of the family and part of their preparation to teach their own children and earn money for their own families later on.

Finally, put a name by each task—working out who will be responsible for each. Parents' names of course will be listed by most of the tasks, and children will go away from the discussion appreciating the fact that their jobs are just a *small* piece of all that the family has to do.

A while ago our family got together and wrote a long list of all the jobs that needed to be done. When I looked at the long list, I realized that my small one or two jobs were not very big at all and that my parents had been doing almost all of the work. Some of them made me realize how many little things my parents have to do every day, things like pay the bills, clean up after we leave for school, just little things like that.

After I realized this I was thinking that I would do more jobs than I already had. Before the meeting I was arguing about how much work I had to do that other kids didn't have to do, but now I realize how much has to be done.

Now we have jobs in the kitchen that we each do after dinner every night. For instance, someone would do the dishes, someone would clear the table, someone would sweep the floor, etc.

We also each got a zone of the house that we need to do

*as often as possible. For instance, I have the bathrooms, Tal-
madge has the living room, etc.*

*We have all of our jobs pined up on a bulletin board so that
we can look at them and see what our jobs are in case we
forget.*

—Noah, 12

As you make up job assignments for your children, be
sure to keep them simple. The more complex they are, the
less chance they have of working.

After we had made our long list of household tasks and impressed the kids with how much there was to do, we tried a
variety of complicated job lists and assignment charts, even a
circular, rotating one that could turn each child's name to a
different job and room of the house each week. Things didn't
work very well until we got it simplified. We found that if kids
just had three things to be responsible for, they had a chance
of remembering and doing them. For example: (1) keeping
their own room tidy (or their part of a shared room); (2)
picking up, cleaning, and keeping tidy one other part of the
house—a bathroom, a hall, the backyard, a coat closet (our
basketball-crazed boys did better when we called their assigned part of the house a "zone"—a place they were responsible for, just as they cover one part of the court in a zone
defense); (3) doing one "kitchen job" at dinnertime—setting
the table, loading the dishwasher, sweeping the floor, etc.

Rather than changing zones or kitchen jobs often, it worked
better to let them stay with one thing or one place for several
months, improving and getting faster at that task.

Our simple chart looks something like this:

Person	Zone	Kitchen
JONAH own room plus. . .	Front hall & closet	Clear table (dishes from table to sink)
TALMADGE own room plus. . .	Living room	Rinse & stack (dishes form sink to cupboard)
NOAH own room plus. . .	Back porch and backyard	Load dishwasher (dishes from cupboard into washer)
ETC.		

Again, it's not a perfect system. Kids weren't always there, and they're certainly not always motivated when they are, but when used with the "peg and payday" program that follows, it surely helps.

—Linda

Earning "Pegs"

Work seems to "work" better when there is some way to signify its completion, whether it's punching out on a time clock, turning in a report, or checking off a finished project on a chart or list. Some kind of accountability or self-monitoring also simplifies the *supervision* of work.

In a family economy there needs to be a clear, workable way for kids to be *aware* of their responsibility and to signify or indicate when they have completed it. We used a simple pegboard to accomplish this. In our system a child has four pegs, each of which represents something he or she is supposed to do during the day. The pegs are an effective way of transferring initiative to children. The punishment for not getting the four expected things done is simply the absence of a reward at the end of the week.

Again, in our family, we learned by trial and error, and again, the answer was simplicity. We'd tried star charts and point systems, but what finally worked best was a simple, blocky wooden pegboard where each child had four pegs. I made the pegs one Saturday afternoon out of two-by-fours and dowels with a drill and a screwdriver and hooked the pegs on with a small chain so that they wouldn't fall off or get lost. Of course a chart to just mark off would work just as well, but it wouldn't have got me as committed.

My homemade pegboard looks something like this:

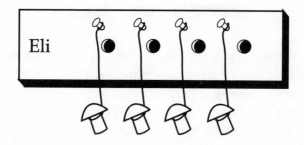

—Richard

Please don't think that you have to be a carpenter and produce your own pegs and pegboard. Many families just buy the simplest multihole commercial pegboard with a jar full of little pegs and set up a board with twenty holes for each of the week's twenty pegs. The board—usually Masonite—will be covered with holes. Just cover all but the twenty holes you need with paper that says the child's name, the days of the week, and numbers for the pegs. It will end up looking something like this:

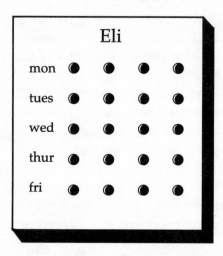

If you don't have the equipment to make any sort of pegboard, try a chart using gummed stars, or just check off boxes on a sheet of graph paper. Whatever you use, try to make it special and different in some way so that your kids will understand that it's important—and will be motivated by just using it.

The first peg is the "morning peg." A child can put it in when he's done what he's supposed to do in the morning or before school (get yourself up and to breakfast on time, make your bed, have a private morning prayer, be ready for school—hair combed, teeth brushed, etc., on time—

whatever things *you* want *your* children to do each morning).

The second peg is the "homework peg," which goes in after school when the day's homework is done (in our case we call it the homework-and-*practice* peg, because those taking music lessons must also do their practicing before putting in Peg 2).

The third peg is the "zone peg," which children can put in after they've tidied or checked their "zone" (area of the home or yard they are responsible for), their own room, and done their part of cleaning up the kitchen after dinner.

The last peg is the "evening peg," which goes in if they get washed and brushed and in bed by their bedtime.

Since homework and bedtime situations are a little different on weekends, the pegs should just be used on *weekdays*. A slightly different approach for weekends is discussed later.

It takes some time and effort to *establish* the practice of using the pegboard or other system—but it *saves* time (and work) over the long run. It is far easier to say "Are your pegs in?" than to say, as so many parents do so many times every day, "Pick up your clothes, make your bed, do your homework, brush your teeth, do your job, practice your piano" . . . and so on and so forth.

There are other ways in which "the pegs" simplify family life. For example in many families a peg system simplifies the decision as to whether to let the children watch television. "No TV until the first three pegs are in" is a good rule that makes TV watching part of the incentive system rather than a given. Incidentally this illustrates the *connections* between a family's legal system and its economic system. You may have rules about the ORDER in which things can be done (first pegs, then TV), and at the same time doing things right (getting the pegs in) can be the basis for an economic reward.

Besides transferring initiative and responsibility to kids, the pegboard system gives parents additional chances for positive praise and reinforcement and gives kids an interesting kind of satisfaction. It feels good to mark your accomplishment by pushing in a big, blocky peg, signifying that you *did* something. At the same time, parents are reminded, by the in-place peg, to give some words of praise and thanks.

I have to tell you that one of the best things about pegs is that your parents bug you less. You would think that they would bug you more—but they don't because you're the one that's supposed to think of stuff and do it. I mean, they might remind you to get your pegs in but it's better than reminding you to do everything.

So it's really good either way. If you do get the pegs in you feel good and you get paid. And if you don't it's kind of like it's your own problem and you don't get paid and you can't do anything and your life just comes to a halt but at least you learn from it and kind of figure it out for yourself.

—Talmadge, 14

PAYDAY

Now, where is the *motivation* for kids to do their assigned tasks each day? Is the physical satisfaction of putting a peg in a hole and the praise of parents enough? Perhaps. But an *economy* needs more tangible rewards—not only for motivation and incentive but to allow the other *parts* of an economic system (the saving, spending, decision-making, and ownership parts) to exist and work.

But this is a sensitive area. If kids are *paid* to do household chores, to take care of their own rooms, to practice a musical instrument, they may begin to do things for the wrong reasons—for money instead of because they are learning to be part of a family, gaining an education or a skill, and becoming responsible for themselves and their things.

But children do need money, and to simply give it to them whenever they ask for it or as an automatic allowance begins to teach them the false principle that they can get "something for nothing" and the false notion that the "world owes them a living." And if they have not *earned* the money they use, they will not perceive ownership of responsibility for what they buy with it.

So what should parents do? Older children may be able to work outside the home and earn money, but grade-school-age children generally can't, and this is the *crucial* age for teaching responsibility and self-reliance.

Again, the answer to the dilemma needs to be simple: Make it clear that the household responsibilities you have listed, the job or zone chart you have made, and the pegboard are *requirements*. Children do their zones and get their pegs in because they are part of a family and that is their share. They are not optional.

What is optional is whether they'd like to *keep track* of how many pegs they get in during the week on daily

95

"slips" and turn those slips in for a Saturday "payday," where they are paid in direct accordance and proportion to how much they have done.

A simple slip, filled in with how many pegs a child got in for the day and initialed by a parent, will look something like this:

A child brings his slips to "payday" on Saturday and turns them in for his weekly pay.

The "household tasks" list, referred to earlier, can be helpful in explaining that everyone who *participates* in the jobs and responsibilities of the family should get some compensation for what he or she does. Dad and/or Mom can work at jobs for money partly because they don't have to do everything at home. All the tasks on the list (from going to a job or to school to taking care of the house) are part of the family responsibilities, and the more a person does, the more he deserves to share in the family's money. In the real world how much you do (and how well) determines how much you earn. It can (and should) work the same way in a family.

"Payday" becomes a brief but important (and weekly) opportunity to reward and recognize and give *attention* for positive behavior. A child who has done well gets a monetary reward along with your praise, while the child who has earned very little essentially gets passed over.

This business, by the way, of rewarding positive and ignoring negative behavior is such obvious and common advice, but it is *rare* to see parents actually practicing it. Stop and watch families in a shopping mall sometimes. The kid who misbehaves always gets the most attention. The child who behaves himself gets ignored. We need to learn to "catch our children doing something right"!

Payday is a weekly opportunity to praise children, elaborately and specifically, for doing well, for being responsible, for remembering, for taking initiative, for being dependable.

In our family one nice by-product that came unexpectedly when we started having payday at our house was the opportunity to do what we all know we should do but usually don't—reward the positive and ignore the negative. I found, as we assembled for payday on Saturday mornings, that I was saying to a kid who'd done well, "Josh, you did great. You got in every peg. You hardly even had to be reminded. Congratulations. Here is your twelve dollars. How did you do it? Do you want it in cash or in your account? Nice going!"

And to another child, "Here's your sixty cents, Saydi."

I could see Josh's satisfaction with himself, motivating him to do it again, and I could see Saydi's resolve not to be so ignored (or so broke) again the next week.

—Richard

Payday should not be an expensive proposal. In most cases it should replace allowances and, as children begin buying their own clothes (see the next section), money that you would have otherwise spent anyway on things your children need.

If you have been giving your children allowances, set the value on each peg so that a child who gets in all of his pegs will earn a bit more during the week than he had been getting for his allowance—and conversely, so that he'll get less than he's used to if he doesn't do well.

For the sake of simplification, when we started the pegs in our family and our children were small, we gave each peg a value of twenty-five cents so that a child who got all four could earn a dollar for each weekday. A child who got all four pegs all five weekdays (twenty pegs) got his money doubled (ten dollars) as a special reward for consistency. As you move beyond replacing the child's allowance, the money amounts you choose should depend on the purchasing responsibilities you give your child (see the section on *spending* money).

Again, each peg represents something a child is expected to do. Because the pegs simplify and clarify tasks, a pegboard, even without a payday, makes parenting easier and transfers some of the responsibility and initiative to kids. Adding a payday increases the child's motivation to remember and get things done.

Give yourself a couple of weeks or more to get the pegboard habit somewhat established. Then, using the reasoning that everyone shares in the household tasks, so everyone should share in household money, explain that those who want to can fill in a slip each night showing how many pegs they got that day, get the slip initialed by a parent (who checks to see that the things represented by the pegs actually got done), save the slips, and turn them in on Saturday for "pay."

Once we got our pegboard and payday system going, we had lots of "fine-tuning" adjustments to make. First we found that the slips would get lost before Saturday unless there was a place to put them. We got a wooden box, cut a slot in the top, and let the kids "deposit" their slips in it. On Saturday, payday began with the ritual of opening the box.

Then we decided that a child who got all twenty pegs (four each day, Monday to Friday) deserved a bonus for consistency, so we paid them twice as much as they'd earned. Then we had kids who got all but one or two pegs begging for a way to get up to the "double" level, so we started putting a quotation or a short scripture on our refrigerator and offering "bonus pay" to anyone who could memorize it. I still remember the first quote—Emerson's "See how the masses of men worry themselves into nameless graves, while here and there a great unselfish soul forgets himself into immortality."

We tried some adjustments that didn't last because they made things too complicated. Once, in an effort to teach self-reliance, we tried a bonus for anyone who got everything done without any reminders or pushes from parents. We learned they all needed reminders. Another time we tried letting one child do another child's job when it hadn't been finished—then required the second child to pay the first on payday. This created too much competition and bad feelings. But the simple, four-pegs-a-day system worked better the longer we used it. Our reminders were seen as help—helping them earn more money (rather than constantly nagging them to do things), and they were competing in an arena where they could all win.

—Richard

It's important to let the peg-and-slip system settle in over time. Try not to push or badger the kids too much. Leave it to their initiative so that they really have the responsibility and the opportunity to "succeed" each week. Let the reward or the absence of a reward each week be their motivation for the next week.

We have somethig caled pegs: At the end of day we rit down how meny pegs we did and put it owr bank. At the end of the weck we have payday. We git our money. The funist thig is payday becus: you got mony and you can sped it or kep it in the bank for callige. Some time pay day is sad becus: sometime you do not get eny mony.

Hers how it fills to put my peg in: I fill relef. in my hart I fill lick I can go wach TV becus my jobs are dun!

—Charity, 7

Charity, as you can see, wrote this the week that her second-grade class was learning about colons (:). Eli also had a little to say on the subject and some of the ways he and his brothers have found to help them *remember* to get their slips filled out each day.

Even though it seems like it would be easy to do slips, it is not that easy to remember to do it every day. The ways how some of us remembers is like put a sign on the front door, put a rock

100

under your pillow, or maybe put a sign on your bed. Some-
times I get five slips at the start of the week and stick them on
my door. Then I just fill one in each day.

Sometimes you forget to do your slip and in the morning
you feel kind of sad because you know that you didn't get
your pegs or your slip. But maybe the next day you try harder
to remember.

Another wierd way to remember that may brother does is
hang up a hanger above his bed on a pipe so he would see it
when he went to bed and remember to do a slip.

—Eli, 10

Other families around the country who use the peg-
and-slip idea have had similar experiences. The system
isn't foolproof, and it can't implemented overnight, but it
is a good first step in shifting responsibility to children and
in setting up a family economy.

OTHER WAYS FOR KIDS TO EARN MONEY

Remember that the goal here is to get money into the
hands of children that they perceive they have *earned.*
Once they have their "own" money—their earned money
—they are in a better position to learn about saving, about
managing their finances, about decision making, and
about ownership and responsibility.

Also, remember that you don't need additional money
in your budget to implement these ideas. Since you're
going to turn over more *purchasing responsibility* to your
children (for example buying their own clothes), the

101

money you pay them on payday or for other things is the same money you would have otherwise used to buy clothes and other personal effects for them.

Because of this you may need to set other ways to allow them to earn money within the family economy. Two of our favorites are a "job auction" for weekends and "deals" for their summer vacation.

SATURDAY JOB AUCTION

In addition to the daily tasks that keep a household going, kids can assume some of the family's weekend jobs—giving parents another opportunity to get "earned money" into their children's hands and free time for themselves. One way to accomplish these weekend challenges is to set it up in a "job auction."

We got so tired of fighting with the kids to get them to work on Saturday (Parent: "Let's get this work done." Child: "It's my only day to play." "Parent: "Work before play." Child: "I've worked all week." Parent: "Someone has to do it." Child: "My friends don't have to," etc.) that we were desperate to try anything.

Friends (who were also trying our pegs-and-payday ideas) told us about their job auction. We tried it and it worked! (Well, it worked better at least than what we'd been doing.)

Not every Saturday, but on weekends when we're home and not too many big events are planned, I make a list of the things that need to be done that day. It usually looks something like this:

1. Mow lawn
2. Trim hedge
3. Clean bathrooms (the bathrooms are one child's "zone," but they still need a more thorough cleaning on weekends)
4. Clean out camping closet

Then we put the jobs up for auction, with each one going to the low bidder. The understanding is that the jobs have to get done by a certain time—say six o'clock that afternoon. One child might bid fifteen dollars to do the lawn and another might underbid him at twelve dollars. Sometimes relatively "fun" tasks (such as trimming the hedge) get very low bids.

It's not quite like they are asking what they can do to help out—but almost.

—Linda

As mentioned earlier, the "peg" system works best on weekdays. Give kids a change of pace on weekends by *not* requiring pegs. But keep your consistency by not allowing them to go anywhere, have friends over, or watch TV until their rooms and zones are okay. Also, a child can't "bid" at the Saturday job auction until his room and zone are tidy.

Summer "Deals"

During the summer while school is out, it may make sense to discontinue the pegs-and-payday system and substitute something less like "piecework" and more like "contract work." Hopefully the good habits developed from the pegs will continue in a more relaxed summer atmosphere.

Have each child put together a list of things he feels he ought to work on or accomplish during the summer. The list should include academic subjects that need attention, but can also include *interests* and things he thinks he would *enjoy* doing. Review the list with him, be sure he understands that each thing on it is its *own* reward but that, as added motivation, you will pay him an agreed amount for each thing he completes. Review the list, add the things *you* want him to work on, and each of you sign it like a contract. Help him plan how much he will have to do each week on each goal to complete it by the end of the summer.

Every summer our family thinks of the things in our lives that we need to work on (for example: basketball, sports, scouts or academic or religious or social goals) or any other things that you think that you need to work on.

One summer our family was about to move, and on my deal one of the things that I had was to make a list of people I was going to write to. After I moved I was so glad that I made that list.

Some more examples of goals on that deal (last year) are: Work on my jump shot until I can make eight of ten, get finished with my Eagle Scout requirements and get so that I can beat my dad at chess.

—Talmadge, 14

Wen we trrn 8 we have to pay for ower on clows. (This will hapn to me next yer.) In the witer, fall and spreg we have pegs and in the summer we have a deal and we get mony for doing

104

*these. Wen we do are pegs we git mony from doing owr gobs.
I lick to ern mony.*

—Charity, 7

*I had a good "deal" this last summer. I got me to remember
the things I was trying to do. I got most of them done and I
saved the deal. Here's what it looked like. [See p. 106.] My
mom said we should be trying to do stuff that would broaden
and contribute. That means you learn some things or get
better at it and you also try to help some other people. So my
deal was things that could do one of these (or both).*

*I won't say how much of this I got done but I didn't do too
bad.*

—Eli, 10

2. Learning to Save Money—The Family Bank

As mentioned, one reason for setting up a family economy
system in which children can earn money is to teach them
the initiative, self-reliance, discipline, and responsibility
that it takes to earn money. A second reason is to give
them the opportunity to learn how to handle money—
how to save, how to budget, how to set goals and plan,
and how to wait for something they want and learn the joy
of delayed gratification rather than the false notion of instant gratification that develops in children who get what
they want too easily. There are three aspects of the "saving" part of a family economy. They are: (a) setting up a
family bank; (b) earning interest; (c) the 10 percent principle.

Eli's Deal
Summer 1993

Broaden	Both	Contribute
1. Read at least 8 books (800 pages). $15	1. Say prayer every night. $10	1. Make a new friend at basketball camp. $5
2. Beat Noah in 2nd platou of tennis. $7	2. Be ready and prepared for Virginia. $15	2. Do my best to hit a home run in Little League. $5
3. Rally 15 with dad. $5	3. Teach the kids in Romania how to throw and catch a frisbe. $10	3. Do my best to pitch a game with only two walks. $5
4. Hit 35 in a row at the backboard. $5	4. Make a friend in Romania. $10	4. Give fifty compliments. $10
5. Beat Noah in a game to 10 (basketball). $7	5. Do several good deeds in Romania. $10	5. Obey the family laws. $10
6. Hit 15 buckets of serves. $5		6. Help Charity get ready for 2nd grade. $5
7. Do my best to make it to the allstars in baseball. $5		7. Do dinner 3 times for mom. $6
8. Make it to the all-stars in baseball. $5	$20 signing bonus Total $190	
9. Beat record in catch with dad. $5		
10. Get 7–10 on free throws. $5	If every one completed bonus of $35 = $225. Goals not met can be made up for by bringing 3 rocks per dollar from beach to designated place on fence.	
11. Learn 3 good songs. $10		
12. Don't lose temper more than 5 times. $15		

Eli (signature)

Dad (signature)

Date

THE FAMILY BANK

In the real world, people save through savings institutions. Setting up a "family bank" into which children can deposit their earnings—complete with a simple entry-and-withdrawal book that keeps track of each of their accounts—can help you teach them the value of saving, budgeting, and spending wisely.

When we decided to start a family bank, we already had a big wooden box that the children used to put their initialed "slips" into each evening. We painted the box gold, carved into its front the words "First National Bank of Eyrealm," put an account book inside to keep track of the kids' totals, and got a big, impressive combination lock to go on it. For a little while at least, the novelty of it (and its impressive appearance) was enough to make kids want to deposit their money.

Our "account book" is very simple. It is just a notebook with a section for each child where deposits, withdrawals, and balances are kept track of. A page looks like the one on the next page.

We keep the account book inside the family bank.

—Richard

The family bank will enhance and breathe new life into paydays, job auctions, and summer "deals" because kids will have a place to put (and to save) some portion of their "earned" money. They can make a withdrawal simply by asking a parent to open the bank, take some of their money out, and reduce the amount in their account book. At the weekly Saturday payday kids now have two options—getting cash or a credit to their account in the family bank (or getting some in cash and putting some in the bank).

Eli		
Date	+ or −	Balance
2 - 3	+ 8.00	116.50
2 - 10	+ 10.00	126.50
2 - 12	− 4.20	122.30
2 - 17	+ 3.00	125.30

Along with the short-term gratification of earning cash for doing their assigned tasks, they can choose the longer-term gratification of watching their savings build and grow.

Somehow I've become a saver. And I've got the reputation among my friends as the one who is always trying to save a little (or at least not to spend it all).

When I try to remember how I got this one good habit I recall how impressed I was with our family bank. I think I was eight years old when mom and dad got it started and I remember liking the idea of having my money there where it was safe, where I couldn't lose it and where I could get it out whenever I needed it. I think I also liked the attention from mom or dad when they wrote my little deposits into our bank and praised me for being "such a good little saver and money manager."

—Shawni, 21

INTEREST

Of course real motivation for saving, separate from what you want to do or buy with your money, is that saved money can grow. Elementary-age children can understand the concept of earning interest and develop saving habits that will help them avoid financial problems throughout their life.

Simply establish an interest rate, explain it to the children ("a bank uses your money, so it pays *rent* on it—interest is rent on your money") and calculate the interest they've earned at the end of each month or each quarter and add it to their total in the account book in your family bank. Explain to them how small amounts, put away regularly and consistently, earn interest that "stays in" and gets more. Interest can grow and grow and give them the money they will need later in life for *big* investments, such as a college education, a house, and so on.

In an effort to simplify our interest system, we made a couple of "too quick" decisions, which ended up costing us dearly! We decided to go with a 10 percent interest rate because the children could learn to calculate it simply by moving the decimal point. But they needed the incentive of getting interest added more than once a year, so we decided to add 10 percent a quarter.

The problem is we have developed a couple of devoted little savers who figured out the concept of compound interest—interest on interest—and quickly realized that their money would more than double every two years. They started saving all of the money they earned! They even tried to borrow money from their friends to put in our bank (obviously paying them a lower interest rate). And one day one of them got an advertisement in the mail that said he'd won a million dollars. He came and asked me if I had $500,000, because I was going to need it to pay his interest that year.

—Richard

Children can help compute their own interest if you keep it simple. Try paying interest once each quarter (at the end of March, June, September, and December). Help them calculate by taking their balance at the end of each of the three months during the quarter, averaging the three, and multiplying that average by the interest percentage you have decided on.

When you think about it, interest is an amazing thing. Money that grows! It didn't take me or my brothers very long to like this idea. We have a little saying someone in the family says every so often. "Poor people work for their money. Rich people's money works for them." I don't think we made that up. Someone else did. But it is true that money can work for you. The problem is that I don't think we're going to find interest this good in most places.

—*Talmadge, 14*

For children not old enough to be intrigued by interest (or capable of calculating it), use a simple alternative. Just tell them that they will receive a *bonus* of five dollars for every hundred dollars they have in their family savings account at the start of each *season* (summer, fall, winter, and spring). As they get older, it will be easy to "convert" this into interest.

Establish a "cutoff point" when children can no longer earn interest in the family bank—when they're old enough to transfer their savings into a regular bank or savings institution.

THE TEN-PERCENT RULE

Not many children are automatic or instinctive savers, even with the incentive of interest. Try to establish a pattern or habit of saving *the first 10 percent* of everything earned. Although it's not always easy to convince children to give up part of that "hard-earned" money, any child who develops this habit is almost guaranteed of a secure financial future.

In the church we belong to, people are asked to tithe—or to donate 10 percent of their income to the church. Early in our marriage, as struggling graduate students, we were finding this extremely difficult and thought about deferring the practice. (I remember thinking that I could keep track of what I "owed" the church and add interest to it and pay it later when we were earning more money.)

Linda and I sat down one evening to discuss the situation and realized that tithing was something we believed in and were committed to. We decided that living on 90 percent of what we earned was just as easy as living on 100 percent—it was just a question of what we were planning on and where we set our limits. Then we became a little upset with ourselves for having considered compromise and, almost as a form of penance, decided to go the other direction. We committed ourselves to paying an additional 10 percent into an investment account for ourselves every month at the same time we paid our tithe—reasoning that the difference between 90 percent and 80 percent was just a question of attitude.

It was the most important financial decision we have ever made. We stuck with the commitment and during the last two years of graduate school saved $2,500—enough for the down payment on our home—a house that is now worth nearly five times what we paid for it.

—Richard

Encourage children who are on the peg-and-payday system to start saving at least 10 percent of everything they earn. Put this 10 percent in a separate column in their account book—treat it as a separate fund that is set aside for investing—that they cannot withdraw for spending needs. Also encourage them to set aside some percentage for a church or charity. Don't *force* either of these. Stress to them that it is their money, that they have earned it and can do what they want with it, but talk about how saved money can grow and about the *advantages* of saving part of their earnings. Help kids realize that the best time to take out a percentage for saving and for charity is right when they get paid.

Another thing I remember from back when we were just starting the family bank and our earning system is Dad's definition of an "investment." It's been 12 or 13 years ago but I remember we talked about an investment being something that would get worth more the longer you kept it. As kids we were trying to think of what that could be. With some help from dad we thought of a savings bond, a house, a college education. I really got the idea of taking one dollar out of every ten and putting it in a different account and never taking any of it out except for an investment.

—Shawni, 21

In the account book inside your family bank have a separate place for these *investment* savings—and distinguish it by having a column *only* for deposits, *not* for withdrawals.

The only difference in the account book is that the investment account has only deposits in the middle column:

ELI (INVESTMENT ACCOUNT)		
Date	Deposit (+)	Balance
9 - 13	1.20	629.13
9 - 20	1.05	630.18
9 - 26	2.06	632.24
9 - 30	29.50 (interest)	661.74

Children will not be using this "investment" capital until they buy a savings certificate or a stock or bond or begin to pay for college. Set up your interest or bonus so that the investment account earns more than the regular account (i.e., if your regular interest is 3 percent per quarter, think of paying 5 percent on the investment account. Or if you opt for a simpler "bonus" of three dollars for every hundred dollars at the end of a quarter, go to five dollars for the money in the investment account.) Let your children put as much of their money as they want in the investment account, so long as they understand that they won't take it out except for an investment. They're sure to make mistakes along the way—overinvesting at one point, underinvesting at another—but the lessons they learn will stay with them for the rest of their lives.

3. Learning to Spend Money Wisely— Budgets and Checkbooks

We usually think of earning and saving as the hard parts and spending as the easy part. But in fact spending wisely, and the record keeping and budgeting that goes with it, is a major challenge for kids (as well as for many adults). And the principles of discipline, planning, restraint, and delayed gratification that are all parts of good spending habits can help children in so many ways.

There are three steps to introducing "spending" within a good family economy. They are: (a) The children begin buying their own clothes and personal effects; (b) they're introduced to budgets and handling cash; and (c) children get family "checkbooks." These steps should be introduced to your kids in sequence—with at least a couple of weeks between each step.

BUYING THEIR OWN CLOTHES

Elementary-school-age children are flattered and complimented by "adult type" responsibility. Telling them that

114

they are now old enough not only to earn their own money but to buy their own clothes and the other things they need is like telling them they are big, they are smart, and you trust them.

As children are given this responsibility, they need to be able to earn enough money to fulfill it. Parents should calculate how much they are spending on a child for clothes and personal effects and then adjust the amounts earned through pegs and payday so that kids can begin purchasing these things themselves.

Be prepared for the predictable fact that your children will make some bad purchase decisions for a while. Minimize this by helping children make lists of what they need. But don't make the decisions for them or force them to buy one thing and not buy another.

We have a daughter whose first purchase after she turned eight was a pair of $75 jeans. I tried to steer her toward less expensive pants and warned her that it was nearly all the money she had, but stopped short of telling her that she'd be sorry or saying, "I'm afraid you're not old enough for this system."

She bought them and enjoyed wearing them for a couple of days and then started wishing she had money to buy some other things she needed.

—Richard

The question parents need to ask themselves is Do I want my children making mistakes and learning from them when they're eight years old and the consequences are minor—or when they're eighteen years old and the consequences could kill them? People really do only learn to be responsible when they have responsibility.

Again, we tend to give kids license too early and responsibility too late. The middle elementary years is the time that children accept responsibility most willingly and the time when mistakes are minor in consequence but *major* in what children can learn from them.

Let me hasten to add that turning over the buying of clothes to children needs a few backup systems. Don't plan on them buying very much underwear or "Sunday clothes" or too many socks. I end up giving items like ties and undershirts as birthday and Christmas gifts. I've even been known to give a pair of socks as a Halloween gift or a Washington's Birthday gift.

—Linda

There are certain predictable consequences of children buying their own clothes, and most of them are positive. Things that have been earned, saved for, and selected by a child will be far better taken care of. Children will become more conscious of what things cost and thus more respectful of other people's property. Perhaps the most important personal consequence for parents day to day is that children will ask them for money less often—and when they do, parents will be in a position to say, "Let's help you earn some," or "Do you want to take it out of your family bank account?" rather than figuring out whether they can afford it.

Back when I turned eight and first started managing my own money it was wierd because I thought it would be hard to

116

raise my own money and buy my own clothes, but after a while I got the hang of going out and earning my own money and buying my own clothes. There was one advantage though that it was that I could buy whatever clothes and shoes, food, anything I would want. 3 questions I ask myself before I buy clothes . . . can I afford it, do I wan't it, do I like it?

I think buying clothes is fun. also managing my own money is great.

—Eli, 10

One thing we do have to tell you: If you have more than one child and you start this system, forget about hand-me-downs! We learned that in a hurry from comments like "Can you have it? What do you mean? I know it doesn't fit me anymore, but it cost me thirty-eight dollars. I'll sell it to you for thirty-six." (Right away we had to have a little lesson on depreciation!)

—Richard

BUDGETS

After children have tried doing their own spending for a few weeks, offer to *help* them by showing them how to do a simple budget. At the start of a month help a child list the things he thinks he'll need that month and then add together how much money he has and how much he can earn (pegs and payday) that month.

Sometimes an "envelope budget" can help. A child writes "new shirt—$30.00" on an envelope and starts putting money in as he earns it until he has enough.

Remember that the saving part (the set percentage to be saved) should be taken out *first*—before other things are budgeted for.

One of our sons, shortly after going "on the system," wanted an expensive pair of basketball shoes so badly that he could hardly stand it, but he didn't have enough money. He asked if we'd buy them for him and we said maybe for his birthday, which was four months away. Then he asked if we'd lend him the money. We said probably not unless he wanted to pay interest. Then he wondered if he could get credit at the store and pay for part now and part later. Finally, having exhausted all of the instant-gratification methods, he sat down and figured that he could earn the rest of the money he needed in four weeks if he did well on payday, and at the Saturday job auction.

He started an envelope budget—"Shoes $103.00." He put in what money he had and worked hard at his pegs. In a month he bought the shoes, which he treated like gold.

The payoff for me came a week or so later when he came in one day after school and said, "Dad, I'm glad I had to save up and wait for these shoes. I think I appreciate them more than most kids do."

—Richard

Sometimes a wallet or a simple purse of their own can help a child keep track of the money they earn. The safest place for it when they're not on their way to buy something is the family bank—where it can be earning interest.

CHECKBOOKS

After you have tried the family bank, interest, and budgets, adding a *checkbook* makes the whole process more fun and more instructional for your child and easier for you. Essentially a checkbook takes the responsibility for keeping track of the child's spending money out of your hands and puts it into his. Just take one of your old checkbooks—with a cover and a check register—and show the child how to use the check register to keep track of how much money he has. Also show the child how to take money out of the family bank by writing a check and how to put money in by using a deposit slip. Deposits need to be initialed in the child's check register by a parent.

What you are really doing is turning more initiative over to him. He is now in a better position to make purchase decisions and to budget or save the things he wants or needs.

If you decide to go the checkbook route (eight-year-olds are usually able to handle it with some patient encouragement and help), then only keep track of their "investment" savings (which they can't withdraw) in the account book in your family bank. They will keep track of the rest in their check register. Each week at "payday" give them whatever money they earn either in cash or as initialed credit in their checkbook register. They can then put their 10 percent or whatever they want to save into their investment savings account by putting in cash or writing a check to the family bank. Now they have two accounts—checking, which they control and keep records on, and investment savings, which you keep a tally of in the family bank. There is always an incentive for children to move their money from their family checking account to their investment savings (which pays a higher interest or bonus).

Three other small suggestions:

1. Since the family bank is really "open" only on Saturdays when you have paydays, encourage kids to

anticipate their needs for the week and keep or take out some cash. (Or, if you are shopping with them, they can bring their own checkbook and write out a check to you, deducting the amount from their check register, so that you can pay for what they buy.)

2. Have a "slot" in the top of your locked family bank so that a child can make a deposit (his check and a deposit slip) into his investment account when you are not there. You can enter it in his savings when you open the bank.

3. Encourage kids to take good care of their checkbooks and to have a special place to keep them since this is what shows how much they have in their account. Then, to be safe, keep a simple total of how much they have for yourself, and update it every week or two just in case they lose their checkbook.

We have never kept much cash in our family bank, thinking ourselves a little like the Federal Reserve—ready to put cash in if a client (child) wants to make a withdrawal. There's usually a little cash in the bank, along with kids' "slips," the savings-account book, and sometimes things the children have put there for safekeeping—such as their baby teeth or old Scout badges.

Once while we were on a short family vacation, burglars broke into our house. Apparently they were interested only in cash because, while they went through everything, they didn't take any electronics, or rugs, or even jewelry. The lock was broken off the family bank and the few dollars that had been in it were gone.

After the shock of seeing the disheveled house wore off a little, we saw a glimmer of humor trying to imagine the burglars looking everywhere for cash, then finding a box with a big lock on it and "First National Bank of Eyrealm" carved into it. They must have thought they'd finally found the jackpot in this apparently moneyless house. We imagined them grabbing the bank, breaking the lock off of it, opening it up . . . and finding baby teeth, Scout badges, and little slips of paper covered with numbers in kids' handwriting.

—Linda

ADJUSTMENTS FOR AGE

Children younger than eight generally are not old enough to do very well with things like checkbooks or interest. But children as young as three can start saving money in their own little piggy bank and can start using a pegboard to keep track of a couple of very simple responsibilities around the house. Parents who have one or more older children "on the system" may find that their younger children want to take part in it too. The best thing to do is to help the younger children anticipate and look forward to their eighth birthdays, when they can start earning their own money, buying their own clothes, earning interest, having a checkbook, and so on, by giving them simple responsibilities and immediate rewards—in a far less organized but still consistent fashion.

In the meantime, perhaps at age six or so, the young child can begin to fill out simplified slips, showing just a number from one to four (showing how many points he got each day), and get a small bonus of perhaps ten cents per day per peg while the older children are receiving their pay on payday.

In our family, when a child turns fourteen, we take him

to the bank and help him open a real checking account. At that point he ceases to have a family-bank checkbook but can continue his investment-savings account in the family bank until he is sixteen (with the idea that the interest he can earn there will help him save for college). When he is fourteen and has a real checking account, he can make deposits by mail (of our checks, which he gets on payday) and write checks at stores that know him.

The advantages of starting a family economy while children are small is illustrated by the reflections of two of our older children. Josh was eight when we started with pegs, checkbooks, and so on, and Saren was twelve. Note the differences in their recollections:

When I was in elementary school, kids would often ask me how much money I got for my "allowance." I was always proud to tell them that I didn't get an "allowance," but that if I got my pegs in every day and put a signed slip in the "bank" every night, that I would get more money than their "allowance." They always thought it was really cool, and so did I.

I can still remember the day dad got the idea of pegs. He was in the workroom for most of the day, and at dinner he showed us his creation. We each had our own board with our name carved in it. There were four holes drilled in each board, with a peg hanging down from each hole. All the boards were chained together, and it was varnished and everything. He explained what we needed to do to put each peg in. We all thought it was really cool. He made a family bank and carved "The National Bank of Eyrealm" on the side. He explained payday and gave us each our own checkbooks for our "family accounts." It was an exciting day. At least I was excited. It made me want to do my job and my practicing, so I could get my pegs in, so I could get some money at the end of the week. We each had our own jobs in the kitchen, and we all practiced instruments. We always looked forward to payday, when we'd get paid according to how many pegs we got in during the week. We got 10% interest every three months. That's 40% a year! I didn't realize how much that was until I opened a real bank account.

Later, mom and dad introduced "zones" (areas in the house that we were in charge of keeping clean). After we had these for a while I slacked off on pegs, which meant I got very little or no money on payday. Maybe I just felt I was too old for it (which I wasn't). It's a mistake I'm paying for, because I would have more money than I do. I can remember my sister Shawni would always get all her points, so I felt kind of bad when I saw how much money she got and I got none.

It's not until now that I realize what a great system it really is! I think my dad is the smartest person in the world, and he's not telling me to say that! I learned so much from this system that will really help me in the future. I need to work hard to be successful. When I look back on our family economy system, I love it! I actually miss it. I wasn't so fond of it at certain times, but it really is a great system.

—Josh, 19

You know, I never really liked "pegs" much when we first started doing it. Now that I think back on the whole idea, it seems to be a very good one. But I didn't like it. I remember when dad first introduced the whole "pegs system" and points and slips and how we would have to buy our own clothes. I felt overwhelmed and put out. I already felt over-burdened by family responsibilities, and it seemed that every kid had nicer clothes than me already. If I had to buy my own, it would be even worse*! I fought against the idea. No other kids had to do so many jobs or earn their own money. I was mad. But you know what? As time went on, I realized that having specific jobs actually lessened the number of things mom asked me to do. My duties were more straight forward. And my rewards were more obvious. And I could pick out my clothes if I had to buy them. And it was pretty cool to figure out your points at the end of the week and get a good bit of money—not just a little allowance like other kids.*

It took a little while, but I began to see the system as a way to have more control, more freedom, not less than other kids. I earned and controlled money, I was a contributing key member of a working economy.

One suggestion I would have for this system is that it be presented very carefully in the beginning—that it be explained as an option resulting in more freedom, more money, more organized family division of labor, more clearly outlined expectations and rewards. People in general react better to ideas and options than to systems which are going to be put in place whether they like it or not.

—Saren, 23

If you are *starting* the system with older children, make sure to take Saren's advice about explaining it carefully. Like all family systems, this one is easier to introduce with younger children, but most older children will go along if you carefully explain the reasons for trying it—and the advantages they'll get out of it (choosing their own clothes, specific limits on their household responsibilities, etc.). Begin with a family bank and family checkbook and go to a real bank after your child has a little experience and is comfortable with using checks and deposit slips.

COLLEGE (AND OTHER INVESTMENTS)

There are few things that worry parents these days as much as the incredible cost of putting children through college. One huge potential benefit of a family economy where both you *and* your children try to put away 10 percent into an interest-bearing account is that these savings will be there when college begins. Remember that the concept of the family economy doesn't depend on any extra or additional income—though that would always be nice. It depends on the discipline you *and* your children show by saving just a little of what you would otherwise spend, and watching it grow.

It works differently for each individual family, but as our children have grown up, we have tried to help them define an "investment" as something you put money into that increases or appreciates in value rather than decreasing or depreciating. So a house or a piece of land or a savings bond would be an investment—and a sweater, a hamburger, or a bicycle (unless you were using it to do a paper route) wouldn't. We've tried to make a pledge together that the 10 percent that each of us saves "off the top" cannot be spent for anything except investments.

Sometimes we've stretched the definition—like the time our nine-year-old wanted to buy a one dollar baseball card which he assured us would be worth fifty dollars in ten years' time (at least he understood the concept).

College qualifies as an investment because it causes one's earning power to increase dramatically. And a child who pays for part of his education with money he perceives as his own because he has earned it (even if he's earned it from you

125

and received the interest he's earned from you) will appreciate a college education more and probably do better in school because he perceives that he's paying for it with his own money.

We have told our children that they have to pay their own tuition at college although we will pay their room and board. This is made possible by two factors: 1) Their savings that have accumulated in the family bank and whatever other form of savings they have, and 2) A family partnership we've put some of our savings into and now owns a little income property and some investments. The children know that they can borrow money interest-free for tuition from this family partnership but that they will be expected to repay it later on when they are able to. (*If* they are able to. We've told them that if a lower-paying career is chosen, teaching for example, or if there are difficult circumstances, the money will not have to be paid back.)

The benefit is that even though it is our money they're using (interest we've paid them or loans from money we've put in the family partnership), they *perceive* it as *their* money, *their* savings, and *their* education. Thus they value it more and apply themselves more seriously.

—Richard

After high school I made an expensive choice—Boston University. It was a carefully made choice because I did have some other options and I knew that I'd be paying my own tuition. I remember doing a sort of cost-benefit analysis. Would a more expensive college pay for itself in higher earnings potential, in a broader, more useful education? The financial consequences of the decision were personal considerations for me.

126

As the "saver" in the family I did have a respectable sum saved up (I'd have had a great deal more if mom and dad hadn't come up with a policy that we could keep our money in the high-interest family bank only until we graduated from high school—the interest was killing them!) and I decided that between my savings and loans from the family I could afford B.U.

I realize now, looking back, that my whole thought process was different (and better) than if I'd had no responsibility to pay for college. And that was just the beginning. I thought about my classes differently once I got there. Since I knew the cost, I knew the value and I'm sure I applied myself more.

—Shawni, 21

Parents' Part

Don't let the *principles* of a family economy exclude *you*. As long as we're teaching children the principle of delayed gratification, earning, and living within means, we should practice the concepts ourselves. Our example will teach children more than our words. We *challenge* you to do three things:

1. CUT UP YOUR CREDIT CARDS.

Nothing does more damage to family economic stability in this country than credit cards. Spending money before we earn it or getting things before we pay for them simply isn't sound financial practice—and it sends a clear message to our children as to what our values really are.

Now that debit cards are available, there is no need for credit cards. The debit card works the same, looks the same, and is accepted everywhere the credit card is. The only difference is that it draws on money already in our accounts, and forces us to keep records of what we spend with a card right along with what we spend with checks.

Consumer debt is just a dangerous and costly business. Credit-card interest rates are three or four times what other interest rates are and with credit cards, impulse purchases of things we really don't need or can't afford are just too easy.

2. SAVE TEN PERCENT YOURSELF.

It may sound impossible, but living on 90 percent of your take-home pay really is as easy as living on 100 percent. It's just a matter of adjusting your expectations—and your budget—to cover *slightly* less spending.

Set up a separate account with a bank, a savings and loan, or perhaps a discount broker, and put 10 percent of each paycheck directly into it. Think of the account as completely off limits for anything other than investments (use the definition we presented earlier—investments can only be things that will appreciate in value).

People who follow this simple formula not only save money, but they develop a greater sense of independence, self-reliance, and confidence. Over the course of a few years even small amounts—consistently saved and invested and left alone so that interest and growth can compound—grow into surprising sums.

And it sets a powerful example for your children.

3. ADOPT AN ATTITUDE OF "STEWARDSHIP."

The concept of "ownership" tends to work against us in a number of ways. If we think of everything we have as *belonging* to us, it is hard to escape feelings of superiority toward those who have less and of envy or jealousy toward those who have more.

Putting too much value on *things* also tends to cause us to de-value, de-prioritize, or at least de-emphasize, in terms of how we spend our time and our energies, *our relationships*.

A healthier and more beneficial attitude toward life's material things could be called stewardship. This attitude recognizes that we don't own anything permanently *except* perhaps our character and our relationships. All material possessions pass through our hands and eventually go to waste or to others. The earth, or nature, or God (depending on how you look at things) is the only real *owner*. We are merely stewards—having the responsibility for, or the use of, or the pleasure of, or the *stewardship* of a thing for a limited time.

This idea can help us appreciate and care for our things without valuing or coveting them to the degree that we want more than we need or that we sacrifice relationships for things or quality for quantity.

Think about stewardship for yourself and talk about it with your children. Help them to *care* for the earth and for their parts of it, to be happy for their stewardships but not envious of the stewardship of others, to realize that how many things you have isn't as important as what you do with them. And help them to see that their stewardships over *things* are not nearly as important as their stewardships over their talents, their relationships, or their potential.

In many ways stewardship is *the* lesson of parenthood. Our children are "ours" not in the ownership sense but in the stewardship sense. They are our most important and most consequential stewardship. And as parents we can give no greater lesson to our children than showing them what stewardship means in a family setting.

The idea of stewardship is the key to our approach to earning, saving, and spending. Our goal in teaching our children about money and finances is not to produce budding capitalists or acquisitive children—it is to produce good *stewards* who will pass the same lessons of responsibility on to their own children.

Second Intermission

Time for another short pause or intermission. Are you feeling overwhelmed? Does the time and effort required to set up a legal system and an economy in your family make you want to give up on them before you've even started? Do your children have problems that seem so serious that family laws and family checkbooks seem trivial and silly?

Well, remember that you don't have to do it all at once. Remember that it will help your family communicate more with one another and will eventually save you time as children assume more initiative and responsibility. And remember that kids experiencing various problems can sometimes overcome those problems as they get more attention from you and as they shift their attention to things you are doing within your family.

And also remember what a *serious* undertaking parenting is and how much it *matters*. What we are trying to do as parents is to create capable, competent, happy human beings. We are attempting to create masterpieces!

This "masterpiece mentality" was poignantly illustrated to me—with visual aids—when I attended a class on painting with watercolors, taught by a prolific and well-known artist. He had displayed in front of the class four large works of art that could not help but inspire the viewer. Before the class began, we novices (and experienced painters alike) were heard to say, "I love this," "How gorgeous," and "What I wouldn't give to have a talent like that!"

In the next half hour this remarkable man sat at a table with a white canvas flat on it and began to create a watercolor before our eyes. After the first five minutes he suggested that we were beholding a painting at its "three-year-old level." Another five minutes brought an eight-year-old, and then an adolescent stage as he added color, shape, and form. To the tune of our "oohs and aahs" he painted what seemed to us a beautiful pastoral scene with a pleasant house and golden field, azure sky and lush trees, flowers and shrubbery, thirty minutes from the time he began.

Suddenly he stood up and compared the picture he had just painted in half an hour to the large masterpiece at the front of the room.

"I know you like this painting because I've heard your comments as I've worked on it." (Indeed one of the wealthier ladies had offered to buy it.) "But what do you think is the difference between this painting and these large, matted, framed, more famous ones?"

Of course we all thought of the obvious answer—time. But his answer was startling: "Hundreds of hours of love." We knew immediately that he was right! We could see the love as he explained that each tiny rose had to be painted around and then filled in. Each masterpiece required a hundred sketches, a certain day, a certain light, a certain mood, a change of thought, and hours and hours of love!

That thought brought me back with a bump to here and now and the challenges I face in parenting my own "masterpieces." His references to his art apply so beautifully to parenting. However, the thousands of hours of love do not manifest themselves on a canvas but in a person. Our "masterpiece" does not start out as a white canvas. The picture has already been sketched when we begin. It probably will not turn out exactly as we had planned, but those hundreds and thousands of hours of teaching, counseling, and creating things like laws, incentives, and family traditions will show.

As our children grow up with their trials and joys, we will have the same doubts this artist did. As they leave our homes, we know that even our friends may never experience the finished masterpiece, nor will many of our children's future friends and associates know "the artists." Yet those countless hours of love will go with them.

And so, as you plunge into the perpetual temper tantrums, horrendous homework, careful counseling, many miscalculations, continuous cooking, loads of laundry, perilous problems, frantic frustrations, and wicked witchery, thinking, "No one will ever know what it takes to raise this child," just remember that there is also great joy in knowing that many will look at your masterpiece and say, "This beautiful piece of art has been loved!"

—Linda

As we mentioned earlier, the reason there are no real "parenting experts" is that every child is different. That's why the family legal system and economy have to be *adapted* according to the nature of the child. That's also why we should be patient and not feel guilty or inadequate if some things take longer to be effective with our child than with someone else's.

"What is wrong with me?" we ask ourselves when we see other smiling mothers around us, apparently floating through their mothering career with children who have clean faces and seem to have never even stomped a foot in anger, while our own world is cluttered with junky closets and screaming kids. We see the "Sunday smiles" of other families and long to be more like them.

I remember a day a few years ago when I took care of a little two-year-old for my neighbor. I have always been astounded by this woman because she gets more done with three little children than I ever could have dreamed of.

I had just spent a particularly grueling time with our constantly crying fifteen-month-old, who was cutting five teeth at once and was dashing out the front door to the street every time someone left the door open for a split second (usually in her birthday suit). When she was "locked in," she spent all her time unloading drawers and putting the contents into the toilets.

Because of my recent hassles I could not believe my two hours with this sweet little two-year-old. Every time I became concerned about her silence, I would dash to the next room, only to find her playing contentedly with a toy. We have never had a child who would play with toys for more than three minutes, but for her it wasn't just a fleeting thing. She played and played, all by herself, with never a complaint.

No wonder her mother doesn't mind taking her shopping, I thought—a task that is at the top of my list of nightmares. By the time our children are two, they are out of the shopping basket in a twinkle, knocking cans off the shelf like a tower of books. The four-year-old is off to find the lady who takes care of lost children, because he loves to hear his name announced over the supermarket sound system.

I learned a long time ago to give very general and sparing advice to parents who ask for help with a personal problem concerning their child. I like to conclude my advice with "Remember, I'm not married to your husband and I don't have your children—spaced as they are in your family—and I don't live in your house or have your mother-in-law."

So often we blame ourselves for our problems with our children or husband when what we should do is realize that every person is different in their own way—and some are more difficult than others. Some children are naturally quiet and obedient while others go through the "terrible twos" from about fourteen months to fourteen years. Some husbands are moody and hard to live with because that's the way their fathers were. And some fathers are gone. Some children are born arguers, and others are natural peacemakers.

Instead of comparing yourself with others and blaming yourself for the problems in your house, realize that every child and every situation is different.

—Linda

As you get ready for this third step, think a little about the true *magic* that is sometimes felt through the love that can exist in families.

I was mad at Richard because he didn't show up for dinner on a summer night when I had planned to take a couple of the kids to see the movie *Sleepless in Seattle.* We left food on the table and dashed off to catch the opening credits.

As I watched the movie, something about it made my anger dissipate, and a strange feeling overcome me. It was similar to the one I felt when I saw *Chariots of Fire, Field of Dreams,* and *An Affair to Remember*—a warm, peaceful feeling that reminded me that there is a certain magic about good relationships. And that miracles do happen, and that there is a certain higher realm to life—guided by a higher source—if we're perceptive enough to recognize it. The kids felt it too.

All the way home the magic aura stayed with us, as I told the children some amazing and funny stories about their parents' dating and engagement that I had never shared with them before. They were things I hadn't thought about for a while. I remembered that I really loved Richard in spite of the fact that I had been irritated over a little thing. I remembered it until we got home.

We rushed into the house, ready to share the magic, only to find a disaster! The dishes were strewn from table to sink. Wet swimsuits and towels adorned the floor—and was I mad! So much for the magic. This was the real world!

"I can't believe that I live with such inconsiderate people," I thought, venting my angry feelings toward Richard, who certainly should have thought of a little "cleanup" even if the kids hadn't. My mind raced through possible reasons for this gross error. I went from "doing dishes just isn't in his consciousness," to "his mother never made him clean up." Luckily Richard wasn't there. By the time he returned home, I was chuckling at myself about the fleetingness of magic. It's such an intangible and impermanent part of our lives. It is as real and as present as the sun, but so often covered and cooled as though by clouds and rain.

Every marriage and family has its own magic. The problem is that the magic comes, not hour after hour and day after day, but in moments. You'll know what I mean when you think back on your own magic moments. Maybe it was gazing into your "partner's" eyes on your wedding day or the magnificent moment of moments when the slippery bluish-pink bundle emerged from his dark watery world to the light of your arms aching to hold him in the delivery room.

Hold those moments—because next comes the colic and

the dirty diapers and the children who at times make you feel helpless and hopeless.

—Linda

Although you can tell from the previous story that all is not always well at our house, the greatest fear we have in writing this book (as we have mentioned) is that you will think that everything at the Eyres' house is just "hunky-dory," as if we have come from "Ozzie and Harriet" homes ourselves, that we are just "breezin' along, singin' a song," doing one family tradition after another.

My father died when I was fifteen, leaving me as the oldest child to help my mother raise four younger siblings. Linda's parents were really two generations older than she. Linda's father, who was born in 1892, was a farmer and hard laborer all his life. He married her mother after he lost his first wife to cancer. He was fifty-one and she was practically a confirmed old maid at thirty-eight. After two years of trying to have a child, they gave up on the natural route and adopted a five-year-old son. Immediately she became pregnant and had Linda at the age of forty-one and her younger sister at age forty-two. When Linda was born, she had a half brother and half sister old enough to be her parents. One died of cancer at forty-one and the other died an alcoholic at sixty-five.

The point is there are no "typical families," and no easy families.

Both our mothers worked full-time out of absolute necessity, and we survived. When we think of formal family traditions we enjoyed as children, unless we think really hard, we are hard pressed to come up with anything other than the typical holiday traditions such as reading the Nativity scene together on Christmas Eve and the occasional family vacation. Both of our parents were just struggling to keep food on the table.

—Richard

As we begin the next section on building a strong family through traditions, we'd like to suggest that traditions are the magic that hold your family together like glue. It is the magic that your children will look back on as their anchor, their connection to something wonderful—something bigger than themselves—a strong family.

Think of your own family traditions when you were a child. If you can't come up with much, try thinking of some of the common, regular activities you shared. Even watching "Gunsmoke" together on Sunday evenings counts. And think about events or activities other than special celebrations of holidays and birthdays. Some traditions are hard to describe or categorize—they may reflect no more than an attitude or mind-set. Sometimes a family tradition is no more than a shared recognition of the importance of courtesy, kindness, love, and service; or appreciation for the fine arts; or gratitude. All of these "values" can be turned into family traditions—even if it's through no more than verbal reminders or incorporation into family activities.

Yes, life is full of irritations such as dirty dishes, arguments, and checkbooks that don't balance. In order for these things not to overwhelm you, make a little magic of your own!

3

Making Magic: Family Traditions

As we sat down to write this third step, we thought it would be the easiest, most fun part of the book—both for us to write and for readers to implement. We would just write up all the traditions our family has enjoyed over the years—list them like a menu—and readers could pick the ones that appealed to them, order them up, and get started.

But as we began thinking about twenty-five years of parenting, of struggling, of traditions that sometimes worked and sometimes didn't, we quickly realized that this wouldn't be like a menu at all. Building a family isn't anything like going to the restaurant. Nothing is ready-made for you. You can't just think about what you'd like and order it.

Rather, family traditions are more like a recipe book. You have to make things for yourself from scratch. You have to think about what your kids will eat, about what ingredients you have, and you have to figure out what to make and how to cook it. And if you want something really special and extra-nourishing, there may be a lot of effort in going out and getting the ingredients and in teaching your children to like something that is new and unfamiliar.

—Linda

And so it is with traditions. First we should be careful about the ones we choose, picking those that nourish values and communication. We must be careful not to overcook or overeat—too many traditions become cumbersome and lose their meaning (and their taste when they are too elaborate or overdone). We need to think in terms of what our children need and what ingredients (time, resources, etc.) we have on hand or can get. And we need to be committed enough to put it all together and to take the time to let it cook.

To introduce this section on traditions, let us share part of a letter from our daughter in Bulgaria that came when we asked her for input for this book:

I love traditions. Anyone in my family can affirm this fact. I've become a traditional traditionalist! All my life I've thrown tantrums over traditions that are dropped or changed or altered in any way. And I've always rejoiced in holidays that are just so, that include all the things I love, all the memories remade and relived every year. I guess one reason I've always been so very attached to traditions is that they give security and create memories. Perhaps the two things that make a family the strongest are security and memories. So I think traditions are vastly important. I could go on forever on this subject—but here are a few favorite traditions.

At Christmas I've always delighted in assigning roles and dressing everyone up as members of Mary's family for our annual "Nazareth Supper." That was always my job Christmas Eve night. How I love sitting around the candlelit table, swathed in sheets and wearing odd bits of cloth on our heads, talking together as if we were Bible characters and laughing as Dad tries to be so serious and Joseph starts teasing Mary and the little kids pick weird names for themselves like "Llama" and "Hiawatha," and everyone complains that they can't see their food and that they hate dates and figs—and "Where's the catsup for the fish?" "Jesus didn't eat catsup." "Really?" Those candlelit scenes will never, ever be erased from my memory.

I love Christmas mornings when Josh always wakes up first—at about 3:30 or 4:00 a.m.—and wakes everyone else up. We all eagerly look in our stockings that Santa leaves on our bedposts and dump out all our candy and treats on the floor in Jonah's room so we can trade toys and candy and feast on oranges and candy canes until we're totally sick—and it's still only 4:30 a.m. Then we all excitedly sit on the stairs singing Christmas carols until mom and dad wake up and appear with messy hair and P.J.s and groggily make us line up to go into the living room—youngest to oldest, or shortest to tallest (I like that way because then I'm nearly at the beginning). Dad goes in and turns on the Christmas tree lights and some Christmas music and finally everyone rushes into the room and searches out presents from Santa with their name on them. We try to be organized—one present at a time—but in the end there's a mad rush of crumpled wrapping paper and kids running around with remote control cars and dolls. Everything's opened before 6:00. Then we have a wonderful Christmas brunch of eggs benedict where there's never quite enough hollandaise sauce or asparagus and we see our cousins and we play our new board games and we fall asleep and we are so together. I could go on forever but suffice it to say—I LOVE CHRISTMAS! And the traditions we have make every member of the family so vital, every moment so dear, every memory so perfect!

I also love birthday traditions. Some birthday traditions really stuck. Others didn't—and that's O.K. On Dad's birthday we always go to a park, rake up huge piles of leaves and jump in them and bury each other in them. For all my life I'll always remember the time we were celebrating Dad's birthday in the leaves and Mom and Dad announced another baby would be joining the family. What joy that was! And I remember one birthday Dad had when we went to the park in the pouring rain and sat together in the van—looking at the wet leaves and remembering together so much we'd shared. Autumn leaves will always remind me of Dad and joy. And I'll always be overcome by an urge to go jump in them!

You know what I really miss now that I'm over here in Bulgaria? I miss the simple things—like coming home from something and just sitting in the kitchen talking to Mom about my day, or taking Charity to the store with me to buy something or hanging out with Saydi, talking about boys and school and friends all night on my big bed. I miss helping Jonah wallpaper his room and having him come put his arm around me. I miss Dad sitting at the kitchen table late at night, telling *me to come sit down by him and talk a while as I walk through. I miss talking to Eli as he sits on the repenting bench about what he needs to tell Dad and Mom so he can get off the bench (he'll be mad at me for writing that). I miss talking to Noah about his girlfriends or having him come give me a hug—just because. I miss Talmadge sticking his head out the door to the garage as I back out in the car, yelling, "Be sure to wear your seat belt!" I miss Shawni coming in my room, early in the morning while I'm still asleep and asking which shoe looks best with her outfit. I miss Josh's gentle smile and I miss him showing me cool things I never would have noticed on my own. I miss long drives home from Jackson Hole or Bear Lake, singing all the family songs or complaining because Dad wants us to sing the family songs or because we're crowded or hungry. I miss laughing together. I miss making cookies with the little kids and eating all the dough before we can get around to baking it. I miss a million other little everyday things.*

All these little things come from the trust *and* love *we feel for each other. And I really believe that all this trust and love comes from the patterns and traditions that Mom and Dad helped us set, the examples they showed us, and the little things we did every day.*

—Saren, 23

There, in a nutshell, are the reasons to work at family traditions—because they offer opportunities to create memories, share love, and build strong bonds between family members. They will not only help your family life be more peaceful and rewarding, they will also give your children memories they can draw on no matter where they go or who they grow up to be.

How Traditions Build Strong Families

A family tradition is a positive "habit" that is both antic-
ipated and remembered. Every family has some traditions,
whether they are aware of them or not. The goal of this
section is to help you think about your traditions, "formalize" or strengthen the good ones, throw out the counterproductive ones, and add some new ones that you like
or think could be helpful.

All lasting institutions (from clubs to schools to churches
to countries) have good traditions that inspire loyalty and
unity and bring their members together. The best traditions are built around shared values and teach and exem-
plify correct principles. They also often enhance
communication and build responsibility.

There are so many different kinds of family traditions.
There are the "big ones" at Christmas or Easter or Hanukkah. There are the crazy things you may have started doing years ago on a birthday and found yourself repeating
each year. There are the annual events your parents celebrated and that you have carried on. There are the little
household habits or patterns that make your home *feel* like
home.

Some families have far more traditions than others.
Some may even have too many. This third step is to help
us all evaluate our own particular situations and to increase the *benefit* we derive from traditions.

In a world that is less and less predictable, in a society
that is less and less dependable, we need to do all we can
to make our families safe harbors in the storm—places
where warm and predictable things happen, places where
our children can develop identities of their own, places

144

and things they can return to (if only in their memories) no matter how far they roam.

Should You Work at Your Traditions?

Shouldn't traditions "just happen"? Do we run the risk of taking the fun and spontaneity out of them by *analyzing* them and turning them into "tools" for changing our children's behavior or values?

Indeed the main reason for family traditions is *fun*, and the simple joy of being together. But family traditions are too important and have too much influence to just "let them happen." By thinking about them and trying to make them the very best they can be, we are acknowledging our children and our homes as our top priority. We are *recognizing* our families as the most important and most *lasting* of institutions. And we are deliberately setting up little "events" that encourage communication and family unity. These traditions will take on lives of their own and will probably continue to influence our children even after we are gone.

Read this section with two questions in mind: (a) Are we getting the most we can out of the traditions we currently have? and (b) What other traditions could we add that would work in our family—that would make memories and teach values?

The Objectives

As with the other two steps, the objectives of Step Three can be diagrammed with a triangle.

We'll look first at a specific list of things that family

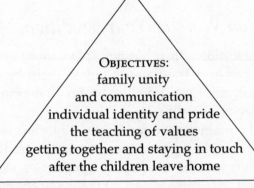

1. Evaluating and Enhancing the Traditions You Already Have

Objectives:
family unity
and communication
individual identity and pride
the teaching of values
getting together and staying in touch
after the children leave home

2. Adding and Refining
(holidays, birthdays, and
other yearly traditions)

3. Family Habits and Patterns
(shorter-term daily, weekly, and
monthly traditions)

traditions can help you teach your children. Then we'll get into the "recipe book" of traditions we've either practiced in our family or been impressed with in other families. Pick the ones that sound good and "nourishing" to you (and that you have the "ingredients" for) and see how they fit into your family.

Finally, we'll talk about the often overlooked habits and family patterns that are often the most important traditions of all.

1. Evaluating and Enhancing The Traditions You Already Have

Some of your happiest memories from your own childhood probably revolve around traditions—things that happened with some regularity in your family.

Most of us would like to create the same kinds of warm family moments for our own children. Or, if we *don't* have those good childhood memories, we want to be sure the same void or empty place isn't re-created in our own children.

The best way to evaluate the traditions you already have is by how they make you feel, how much they pull you together, and how much your children remember and anticipate them.

Another way to evaluate them is to think about what they actually *teach* your children.

In this section we identify eight key aspects of life that family traditions can help your children understand. Use this list of elements as a yardstick to assess your own family traditions. We'll use them to help identify the benefits of other traditions that we will suggest in the two sections that follow.

Eight "Basic Benefits" to Look for in Family Traditions

Today many good recipe books include what each serving will give you in terms of calories, fat grams, vitamins, and so forth. As we decide what traditions we want to continue cooking and serving up in our families, we need to pay attention to what's in them and what we get out of them.

The first criterion for a good tradition is simply that it brings family members together, strengthening the ties that bind us to each other and making joyful memories. Every tradition that does this is worth keeping regardless of whether it does anything else. In fact another definition of a good tradition is "a practice or habit that unites family members and enhances their joy."

There are at least eight other aspects of life that family traditions can help us to understand and develop. Let's look at them together and then define them one at a time.

VALUES	RESPONSIBILITY
COMMUNICATION	SENSITIVITY
EDUCATION	INDIVIDUALITY
MARRIAGE	GUIDANCE

VALUES: All good traditions, by definition, promote certain values, such as loyalty and unity. Certain traditions directly promote a particular value—for example, many Christian traditions reinforce generosity.

COMMUNICATION: Many traditions can improve communication between family members.

EDUCATION: Some traditions can improve your children's education—by reinforcing ideas or concepts they are learning in school or in many cases introducing history, values, or ways of thinking that schools leave out.

MARRIAGE: Some traditions, when practiced in two-parent families, can strengthen the marriage relationship and partnership.

RESPONSIBILITY: Some traditions help improve children's (and adults') abilities to accept responsibility, to set goals, and to be independent and self-reliant.

SENSITIVITY: Some traditions increase family members' tolerance, empathy, and respect for others.

INDIVIDUALITY: Some traditions increase children's sense

of individual confidence and uniqueness, help with their sense of identity, and offer parents opportunities to praise their individual gifts and unique talents.

GUIDANCE: Some very special traditions have a certain "light" or "magic" about them—and may invoke a spiritual connection, guidance, or direction from a higher power.

DECIDING WHICH TRADITIONS TO KEEP

Take a few moments and list any traditions you can think of in your family. You'll think of more as you read through the next two sections and see suggestions that are similar to things you already do. For now just list the ones that come immediately to mind. Then think about whether each one brings unity and joy to your family—and which of the eight principles it helps your kids to appreciate and understand.

For example maybe you color Easter eggs on Easter. This brings the family together and you have fun. Maybe family members show real *individuality* in how they do their eggs. Maybe a lot of *communication* happens as part of deciding who gets to use which egg dye. Maybe you talk about *values* and the true meaning of what Easter celebrates.

Or perhaps you take a short vacation to the same place each year. Maybe a certain child has a particular *responsibility* for packing or getting ready for the trip. Maybe there's some *education* involved—in preparing routes, stopping points, and so on, or in learning about the place you're visiting—or some *sensitivity* can be developed for a

149

person you go to see or for the environment of a place you visit. And maybe there is a lot of *communication* as you drive.

Write down which of the eight principles each of your traditions helps your children with (or that it *could* help them with if you made certain adjustments). Based on this exercise, decide which traditions you want to emphasize and concentrate on, which ones you want to continue to invest your time and energy in. If you find traditions that reinforce *none* of these elements, you might want to consider abandoning them. This rarely happens, since most totally unrewarding family traditions tend to extinguish themselves. However, you may find aspects of your traditions that you'd be better off without—for example overeating at Thanksgiving, or overimbibing on New Year's Eve—because they actually inhibit or lessen the likelihood of principles on the list.

2. Adding and Refining: Holidays, Birthdays, and Other Yearly Traditions

Now, in addition to staying with (and improving) the recipes we already like, it's nice to try a few new dishes, or some variations to the ones we're used to.

The traditions listed in this section are well tried and tested (and "tasted") and they are "coded" according to the "beneficial ingredients" they contain (which of the eight principles they can help children with).

A lot of them are our own, but we've certainly never

tried to do all of them all the time. Be careful not to try to do too many. Sometimes, when we read through a recipe book, especially when we're hungry, almost every dish looks appealing or tasty—but remember that you can't eat them all at once. Pick only the ones you will enjoy the most (and can realistically do). Remember that your best traditions will be your own unique ones, that you evolve or develop yourself. Let this recipe book give you ideas for your own personal recipes.

BIRTHDAY TRADITIONS

| COMMUNICATION |
| EDUCATION |
| INDIVIDUALITY |

Most of us have *general* traditions that center on birthdays—gift giving, birthday cakes with candles, making a wish before blowing them out, parties, and so on. But if each individual child's birthday is connected to a special or unique tradition, it can become even more memorable and fun. And when a tradition is built around the birthday of a particular child, that child feels honored and special.

As our children have grown up, two different kinds of recurring traditions have developed. One has to do with what we do each year on a given child's birthday (usually according to the season it falls in).

Saren's birthday (July)—go to a beach.
Shawni's birthday (January)—build a snowman.
Josh's birthday (January)—go sleigh riding.
Saydi's birthday (August)—float her cake. (This one re-

151

quires a little explanation. We read a Tasha Tudor book once about an old New England tradition of floating a birthday cake with lit candles down a little stream at night. Then they would retrieve the cake, blow out the candles, and eat it together. Saydi was so intrigued with the idea that it became her birthday tradition. Now, every August 12th, wherever we are, we have to find some body of water to float her cake on. We've floated it on lakes, on irrigation ditches, in swimming pools, and one year, in a real time crunch, in the bathtub.)

Jonah's birthday (April)—fly kites.

Talmadge's birthday (February)—make valentines.

Noah's birthday (November)—go bowling. (Don't ask me why—it's just something he loves to do.)

Eli's birthday (July)—water ski.

Charity's birthday (June)—have a barbecue and dance.

Dad's birthday (October)—rake a big pile of leaves and jump in them.

Mom's birthday (April)—go on a picnic.

Some of our birthday traditions have "caught on and taken hold" better than others. It seems that the more unusual they are, the more the children look forward to them and make sure we do them. For example we never miss Saydi's (floating the cake) or Dad's (jumping in the leaves).

The second kind of birthday tradition that has grown up links the children together through a common experience when each reaches a particular age. We've developed a tradition of making a different-shaped birthday cake for each year. When children turn one, they get a round birthday cake. When they are two, it's a cake shaped in the outline of an elephant. Three is a castle, four a clown, five a bear, six a little girl or boy, seven a cat, eight a church. There is nothing particularly significant or symbolic about these shapes. In fact they are just what Saren, our oldest, chose on each birthday. Shawni, the second, wanted the same shapes, and a tradition was born.

What's fun now is to look back through birthday pictures and put together and compare the children with their clown cakes (four years old) or their cat cakes (seven).

—Linda

I think my birthday tradition is one of the strangest we have. Every August 12 my family and I go and float my birthday cake. I have no idea why or how I got this odd tradition—but it's fun and exciting. We are usually up at Bear Lake in Idaho and we find some sort of float to set the cake on and whether the water is wavy or calm we set it down and let it go. Not once to this day has it gotten one drop of water on it. I remember one time it was a stormy day and the waves were higher than me (I was little). I faithfully walked it out, set it in and ran back to the shore—hoping it would somehow stay on the little rubber air mat. Sure enough, it floated in without getting a drop wet.

On my 12th birthday we had a major dilemma. We were stuck in the city for my birthday and there was no place to float it. Since the bathtub was too small (I had a big cake that year) we took it out to Raging Waters, a water park, and floated it in the wild wave pool. The weird stares and odd comments made this birthday tradition especially memorable.

—Saydi, 18

ANCESTOR BIRTHDAY PARTIES

VALUES
EDUCATION
INDIVIDUALITY

One valuable but often overlooked source for building children's positive identity and self-image is their *ancestors*. Children who know a little about their grandparents or great-grandparents can come to understand that they are descended from these people and that the qualities or talents or good characteristics of these ancestors can be passed on and can be a part of their lives now. Write down any stories you know about an ancestor that shows courage or honesty or some other good trait. Get hold of any photos you can find. Then, on that ancestor's birthday, make a birthday cake, have a little party, and read the stories or reflections you've written about his life and character.

We have a book in our family called the Ancestor Book. It has stories, pictures and much more information on each and every ancestor we have.

I like to hear these stories because, in a way, they are about me. I mean I came from them so I'm kind of like them. And it helps me to know what things were like back then. Also, if you have a birthday party for them you get a lot more partys and a lot more cake.

This book gives alot of information on our ancestors and our family traditions. I highly recommend it!

—Eli, 10

Get help with this "ancestor tradition" from other members of your extended family. Share genealogical informa-

154

tion, photos, copies of ancestors' journals, and so on. If your family hasn't done much genealogy, split up the research opportunities within your extended family; do some looking and then some sharing. Various civic, governmental, and church libraries of archives have a surprising amount of information. And with computers it is easier than ever to access. The Mormon church (Church of Jesus Christ of Latter Day Saints) has branch genealogical libraries all over the country that are free to the public and that tie in to the most extensive genealogical research data base in the world.

CHRISTMAS TRADITIONS

VALUES
COMMUNICATION
EDUCATION
SENSITIVITY
GUIDANCE

Note: Because of our own family background, most of the traditions we've suggested for Christmas have a Christian religious flavor to them. Of course families of many different religious and ethnic backgrounds celebrate Christmas—and each family should pick from the broad range of activities available to find the one that suits them. Rather than cataloguing the scores of Christmas traditions that exist, we think it's best if you first look into the traditions popular in your own family background—to emphasize family continuity from generation to generation—and then research and experiment with new traditions that might work for you.

As families become more mobile and as the pressures and complexity of everyday life seem continually to increase, we become more and more appreciative of the "traditional" year-ending holidays of Thanksgiving and Christmas or Hanukkah. For many families the holiday season *means* tradition. It is the one time where there is an effort made to cause things to happen the same way as they have in past years. As roots and stability get harder to find, we sometimes cling almost desperately to the memory-laden holiday traditions we grew up with. In fact some studies show that one of the most common factors causing marital discord (particularly early in a marriage) is arguments about which traditions (his or hers) to carry on with at the holidays.

I remember our first lonely Christmas together—just Linda and I in a tiny student apartment in Boston, very much in love and happy to be together but missing our families out West and flooded with the memories of Christmases past.

We went out on Christmas Eve, when prices had been reduced, got the only little stick of a Christmas tree that we could afford, and brought it back to decorate. Back home my family had always painstakingly hung thin tinsel straight down from every inch of every branch. To me it was a labor of love, the essence of preparing for Christmas, creating an orderly, shimmering tree. Linda's family had "bubble" lights on the tree and left most of the green showing—she couldn't imagine doing it any other way.

What an argument we had! And how important it seemed!

—Richard

The trick of course is to combine and merge the best traditions from both extended families and to add unique ones of your own. The best family Christmas traditions bring families together in a spirit of warmth and mutual appreciation, they enhance both our appreciation and our desire to give, and they create great "photo opportunities" and other memories. Some "prototypes" are listed here that may be useful as you consolidate and refine your own list:

CUT YOUR OWN CHRISTMAS TREE. Whether it's in the woods or at a tree farm, there is something about going out as a family and cutting it yourselves that can help cut through the cloud of commercialism that surrounds the holiday.

The Christmas tree is important to many of us. One thing we have always tried to do is to cut down our own Christmas tree. It started when we lived in Virginia and went with us to Salt Lake City but we could never find a place to cut one down. About three years ago we heard about this place not too far away that was great for fresh cut trees so we traveled there about two weeks before Christmas. It was hard to find but we figured it would be worth it.

As we arrived we quickly figured out that the owner of the trees was not home so we decided the next best thing would be to visit a neighbor. He told us to just cut them down and he would tell the owner and have him bill us. It was a frozen-toe night with snow falling lightly in the pine forest. We had to ask for a saw from the neighbor since we forgot ours. He gladly gave us one and we looked for a long time to find the perfect tree because with 11 people, including Saren who thinks she knows everything, it isn't easy to choose two trees. They had to be just perfect in every way.

No one had any boots on, the happy spirit we had on the

way was fading quickly. The trees were finally chosen and stuffed into the back of the truck. We returned the saw and headed for home. The bill came for the trees and was much more than expected but the experience we had made it worth every cent. Besides, I didn't have to pay for it. Even crazy experiences many times turn out to be great memories.

—Jonah, 16

Straws in the manger. Some Christian families put a small wooden replica of a manger on their mantle or table in early December with short lengths of straw nearby. Family members, particularly children, place a straw in the manger each time they do a good deed or an act of kindness. Hopefully by Christmas Eve the manger is full of straw and soft for a small doll or representation of Jesus that is placed in it that night.

Buying and wrapping their own. In the struggle to help children think of giving rather than getting at Christmas, it helps to have a shopping day with them where they can select and buy gifts for others with their own "earned money," even if the shopping is done at the five-and-dime store. A small child who picks out a $1.59 potato masher for his aunt and wraps it himself is much more likely to anticipate and feel the joy of giving than one who does nothing but think about what he wants from Santa.

Children's gift giving on Christmas Eve. Another way to emphasize giving is to separate the "Santa stuff" from the family's gift giving to each other. Many families give gifts to each other on Christmas Eve, when the focus can be on the individual children and their gift giving. Focus your praise, thanks, and *attention* on each child while he gives out his or her gifts.

Even as we look at these ideas for Christmas traditions, we warn you again that deciding on just one or two is important. Christmas can easily turn into one of the most frustrating times of the year, with its demands for festive food, decked halls, and massive gift giving. Maybe this is the year to start a tradition of cutting back!

Often Christmas brings feelings of guilt, stress, and depression—especially when your kids are misbehaving and it seems like everybody else's are perfect.

Last Christmas as I finally found time to read the mail and catch up on the newsletters pouring in about all our friends' "perfect" children's accomplishments, I read one that was an absolute showstopper:

Jennifer simply loved her study-abroad experience. She absolutely inhaled the sights and sounds of ancient and modern Europe. She had a starring role in *Camelot* and still finds time to sing in vocal groups, play in the civic symphony, and hold down a part-time job.

Alex graduated from Viewmont High School as a student-body officer and attended Boys' State. He recently received his Eagle Scout Award. He'll be touring with a dance company next summer, playing his banjo with a live band.

Jan is an excellent student. This year she resumed her study of piano (along with mandolin and cello). She is on the tennis team and also excels in softball and basketball.

Joseph started high school this fall and has participated in many school and community plays. He has been to

Disneyland this year twice (with choir and Youth Symphony). He is great at cutting hair and was chosen as sophomore "Preferred Man."

Elizabeth has scads of friends who call her every minute to see if she's still breathing. She's a great babysitter and is developing her talents in violin and clogging. She is repulsed by modern music and much prefers the "oldies" radio station.

Jared is studying the banjo and piano. He is also very good in singing and all sports. His last year's Knowledge Bowl team won, partly due to the fact that he could identify the flag of nearly every country in the world.

Allison is in the finals for the third-grade Knowledge Bowl team. She takes lessons in piano and clog dancing. She's also in the University Children's Dance Program.

Louise is dramatic and artistic, is continually cutting, pasting, and sewing and participated with her brother in the Children's Chorus for *The Nutcracker,* and studies clogging and modern dance.

Theodore was interviewed about the problem in the Middle East on a local radio station recently along with the other children in his class. I was so glad we had talked about it, so he had an opinion.

Our baby, Kelly, is a joy! She has a wonderful imagination and makes up names for everything she has and can play alone for long periods of time with only tiny toys and her imagination.

We love you all—Merry Christmas!

My reaction was to look up and say, "This is sick! How can one family possibly do all this?" I decided that they must be working with a very different gene pool than ours!

I would like to send out a Christmas letter some year that tells it like it really is. It would go something like this:

Josh procrastinates until it drives us crazy! He's always screeching in at the last second, making the deadline by a hair or missing it by a hair.

Saydi is "Miss Sweetness and Light" to her friends, but mostly cries and whines about how far behind she is and how tired she is when she's at home.

Saren never has good, reliable friends. She always feels betrayed and left out.

Jonah made a deal with us that if he got a 4.0 GPA, he could quit piano lessons—which, to our amazement, he did—for the first time in his life! (The joke, however, is on him, as I was about to make him quit. After three years of lessons he's still not sure which way is up and which is down on the piano.)

Shawni is so homesick at college that I think I could actually detect green around the ears in the last snapshot.

Talmadge would rather die than do his homework, and often actually forgets it on purpose. He has to be taken by the hand and "sat by" to keep him on track.

Noah cannot stand to lose an argument and is incapable of stopping his mouth before he gets himself into trouble.

Eli has a terrible temper, is a perfectionist, and consistently runs away from home (I help him pack).

And our sweet baby, Charity, runs the household. She's a disaster a minute. When she says "Jump!" we say, "How high?"

P.S. At least four of our nine children have not yet learned to flush the toilet. We're not certain of the number, due to the predominance of "Mr. Nobody" around our house. We love you. Merry Christmas!

—Linda

SANTA WRITES BACK. Add a new twist to letters to Santa by having him reply by letter. Encourage children in their letters to ask Santa about Mrs. Claus, about the reindeer, about his health. His return letter can praise them for their thoughtfulness—for example, "Most children just ask me for things. You were so kind to ask how I am doing.". . . and so on. (Incidentally so many parents worry too much about the "deceit" or "untruth" in the Santa Claus tradition. Rather than worry, just do two things: (a) Emphasize frequently, if you are Christian, the *real* meaning of Christmas; and (b) let children tell *you* the difference between "real" and "imaginary." Explain very simply that some things are *real*—they really happened, they really exist— and that other things are *real* and *wonderful* in our *imaginations* and that "imagining" is fun but not the same as real. Then ask if they can tell you which are "real" and which are "imaginary": the Little Mermaid, the Easter Bunny, the president of the United States, Santa Claus, Moses, the Tooth Fairy, Jesus, Aladdin, and so on. You'll find that children age five and over can make the distinction—and can live with it so long as you assure them that "imaginary" is still *important* and *fun* for you as well as for them.

TRIP INSTEAD OF PRESENTS. Some families, longing for an escape from the hassle of shopping and "I want this" mentality, have found that for the same money they've spent on toys and other things no one really needs, they can take quite a nice family trip where communication and togetherness can take priority over busy stores, selfish attitudes, and social events every evening.

Compare what it might cost for a week in Hawaii or Mexico or some other warm place (there are some bargains). If you go to a place like Mexico, there may also be opportunities to give simple gifts to an orphanage or a poor family on Christmas.

CHRISTMAS EVE CAR RIDE TO LOOK AT CHRISTMAS LIGHTS. Sometimes in the rush and bustle of Christmas Eve, it's nice to get out of the house for a leisurely drive to look at Christmas lights and decorations in your neighborhood or in the downtown area.

READ TOGETHER. Many families have the tradition of gathering around the tree on Christmas Eve to read the Scriptures or to read a favorite classic Christmas story, such as *A Christmas Carol* or *The Gift of the Magi*.

THANKSGIVING TRADITIONS	
	VALUES
	COMMUNICATION
	EDUCATION
	SENSITIVITY
	GUIDANCE

THANKSGIVING CARDS. Try sending handwritten Thanksgiving cards instead of Christmas cards. There are several advantages:

1. Thanksgiving lends itself to a simple message, written yourself, to friends and family—essentially expressing your gratitude for them.

2. Most people are a little less busy just before Thanksgiving than just before Christmas.
3. You'll get more Christmas cards than ever before because everyone who gets your Thanksgiving card will feel obligated to send you a Christmas card!

THANKSGIVING THANKFUL LIST. Get a roll of cash-register paper and make a numbered list of things family members are grateful for. One family member, acting as scribe, lists everything anyone in the family says—"pianos," "hot dogs," "dogwood trees," "our new driveway," "freedom," "perspective," "CDs," "the fall of communism," "lower mortgage rates," "monarch butterflies," "rain," and so on. In most families the list will be rather long, and a certain group dynamic will operate as minds shift to different categories of blessings.

If you have a Thanksgiving prayer or blessing on the food at your Thanksgiving meal, give thanks (collectively) for all the things on your list.

THANKSGIVING HELP FOR THE HOMELESS. Either in place of or in addition to your own traditional meal, bring food to a shelter on Thanksgiving Day—or invite homeless people, a less fortunate family, or people from a foreign country to come to your home and eat with you.

DRESS UP. It doesn't take much (a few feathers and pilgrim hats) for children to get in character for Thanksgiving, and perhaps to reenact Indians meeting settlers and sharing their food. It's much more fun if parents dress up too.

Again, the *longevity* of the family traditions you start is illustrated in a letter from Saren about her first Thanksgiving in Bulgaria:

We tried our best to cook ourselves Thanksgiving dinner. For a turkey, all we could find was two halves of a chicken—so we tied them together with a hanger and baked them. We made mashed potatoes but we had nothing but yoghurt to put in them, so they turned out tasting—interesting. We had a lot of opinions on how to make gravy. Oh, mom, our rolls were terrible. They rose and fell and turned out very rocklike. I'll never make fun of your rolls again.

I made everyone tell me what they were thankful for and wrote it all down on a list—everything from heaters to public rest rooms to ovens that sometimes work. I also made everyone wear pilgrim or Indian hats. It was quite a hilarious scene—everyone in funny paper hats, crammed into a tiny Bulgarian kitchen discussing what they were thankful for and the constitution of gravy.

—Saren, 23

TRADITIONS FOR OTHER HOLIDAYS	VALUES
	COMMUNICATION
	SENSITIVITY

There are so many! Again the best ones are those that have evolved in your own family. Here are a few memories from our family that may stimulate you to expand or enhance your own:

All our children, especially when they were small, loved April Fool's Day—from Saydi, who used to start out yelling that there was a huge spider on her sister's back, to Josh, who always put a rubber band around the handle on the sprayer in the kitchen sink so that the first person who turned on the tap got sprayed on the face.

On Easter weekend we go to a man-made lake and camp on a sandy beach where the Easter Bunny always comes at night to hide the eggs the kids have colored the day before. One year a coyote also came during the night, and all the kids found was dozens of eggshells and lots of tracks.

On Valentine's Day we run around the neighborhood, leaving valentines on porches, ringing the doorbell and running away so that people just find the cards when they come to the door. One card has a nearly invisible thread tied to it so that one of our kids, holding the other end of the thread as we hide in the bushes, can give a little jerk and make the valentine "jump away" just as someone tries to pick it up.

On Halloween, in addition to school festivals and costumes, we set up some loud "scary music" and let the very young children who don't go trick-or-treating dress up at home so that they can "scare" the kids who come to our house.

On Mother's Day several years ago eight-year-old Shawni, something of a natural artist, made a big poster for Linda on which she'd drawn the whole family, with cartoon-style "balloon loops" above their heads saying what that person says most often. Linda, on that first card, was saying, 1. "Get in the car, we're late"; 2. "Where are your shoes?"; and 3. "Where is my purse?" The kids in the picture were saying things like "Josh hit me" and "I'm telling." There was such honesty about the whole thing that we all laughed for an hour. Since then every year Linda is presented with a new poster on

Mother's Day containing the latest versions of what everyone is saying.

—Richard

Halloween is always a great time of year and the most memorable part for us is carving pumpkins on the Monday night before Halloween. Sometimes no one could wait that long so we would do them two weeks early and many times the pumpkins would get rotten before Halloween came.

We all go to the grocery store and have everyone pick out a pumpkin for each, in proportion to all of our size . . . sometimes ending up with about two hundred and fifty pounds worth of pumpkin. At home the table is covered with newspaper and a big bowl is set in the middle for all the seeds and iky stuff from inside. First the faces are drawn on and the tops cut off, then they are cleaned out as much as time allows, and the faces are carved (many times being goofed up and changed from one creature to another). Everybody does their own—completely. After everyone has finished, all of the wild creature pumpkins are set on the window seat in the greenhouse for everyone to see.

Prizes are always given out to every pumpkin. I often wondered how so many prizes were found. A particular prize was made up for each one and many times that took a lot of creativity. The prizes ranged from "scariest" to "most spontaneous" to "weirdest" to "stupidest" to "biggest" and so on. Dad said they were like people—every one different but each the best at something.

Carving pumpkins has always been a great tradition and I'm sure it will live on through my children's children.

—Jonah, 16

Family Vacations

COMMUNICATION
EDUCATION
SENSITIVITY

Too often family vacations are more stressful and hassled than our regular schedule. We try to plan and do too much, to travel too far, and to have too much "fun."

For families that have children at home, the best vacations are often the ones that just get the family away together—away from friends, away from the distractions of home, away from the hectic pace and schedule of the usual.

As a young boy the tradition I remember most was our yearly summer vacation. We would usually go to some wild, isolated place where we'd be forced to be together and "communicate." Sometimes this bugged me at the time (being away from friends) but I admit these experiences were memorable. The most memorable for me, even now, is our trip to Oregon at the age of eight, where I learned the true JOY of work along with the importance and need for work. The Blue Mountains of Oregon (near Pendleton) were totally secluded with only the family and a lot of work to build our log cabin with a chain saw with no electricity or running water. We all become better friends with each other by going on hikes and working together to get the highest logs stacked upon each other to make the 16 × 16 little cozy cabin with a loft (little house on the prairie style). I am not quite sure how it happened, but working actually became fun and exciting. To this day Oregon is my favorite place to go with my family and to be able to do more work on the cabin is a privilege.

—Jonah, 16

One of my most memorable times with my family was when we floated down part of the Snake River. We had a great time. It was me, my dad, and my four brothers.

We saw a lot of wildlife while we were floating down the river including 2 bald eagles.

It was a really long time ago—about 2 years I think. But I can still remember it.

We had to get out at times and push the boat because it was really shalow. It was really deep in other places and me and my older brother, Talmadge, hung onto the boat and got in for a minute and it was freezing!

We also ate lunch while we were floating down the river.

After we had been on the raft (inflatable raft) for a long time there was a place where my mom picked us up and we went back to civilization.

The best thing about that floating, now that I think about it, was all the talking we did. We were just sitting there in the boat and there was no TV and no place to go really. You couldn't get up and walk off. So we just talked about every-thing. You'd be surprised how fun that is.

—Noah, 12

The interesting thing is that exotic vacations don't cost very much. The cost of the Oregon experience was just the gas to get there and the food we ate. The same with the river trip (we borrowed the boat). Even the experience in the Philippines that Talmadge writes about below was ac-complished with airline frequent-flyer miles that we'd saved up for years.

The vacation that I remember most was our trip to the Phil-lipeans. We went there about 3 years ago. And it was such a great experience for me.

I was reading threw my journal last night. I found that I had writen a lot on the Phillipeans.

In my journal it said, "The first day that I was there we drove threw the capital city (Minnila). There were no real houses, just shacks and cardboard boxes. I learned so much there about how lucky we are as Americans to live here. We were in the city for two days and also saw Smokey Mountain which is just a huge pile of garbage that over 20,000 homeless people live on.

—Talmadge, 14

One vacation that *did* eat into our savings was a trip to Romania and Bulgaria to visit Shawni and Saren, who were doing humanitarian service and missionary work there. Even then the only cost was airfare because we had some free tickets, and the food there (what there was of it) is extremely inexpensive. And the trip was worth it just for what Charity learned:

Wen I lernd somethig on a family akashin. Well, it was wen we wint to Romenea and Blgerea. I lernd to not be sefis for thigs I do not ned becus the pepl ther do not evin have good clothin.

—Charity, 7

Family "Majors and Minors"

VALUES
EDUCATION
SENSITIVITY

In September, as a new school year starts, sit down as a family and decide on two things to concentrate on *together* as a family during the year ahead. Pick one important thing (perhaps the study of a foreign language, or of Scripture, or of music, or of the genealogy of your family) and one "lighter" thing (trying to learn to play tennis, going camping, telling jokes, or developing a sense of humor). Designate one as your family "major" for the year and the other as your family "minor." Doing this—especially in discussion with your child or children—can give you something to work on together (or at least to be conscious of together and talk about) throughout that whole year.

Looking back through our list of "majors and minors" brings back some great memories. We didn't always spend a lot of time at them, but they gave us a little bit of united *focus,* and they were always chosen because they were related in some way to the events or circumstances of a particular year.

	Major	*Minor*
1980–81	music	sports
81–82	art	China
82–83	education	tennis
83–84	Spanish	Mexico
84–85	friends	fiction
85–86	charity	humor
86–87	harmony (singing)	horses
87–88	writing	chamber music
88–89	service	Utah
89–90	leadership	wilderness exploration
90–91	Japan	bad backs
91–92	contribution	politics
92–93	values	Eastern Europe
93–94	current events	volunteerism

—Linda

"WELCOME THE SEASONS"

EDUCATION
SENSITIVITY

If you live in a place where there are distinct seasons, it is fun for children to anticipate the flowers of spring, or the snow of winter, or the bright leaves of fall. Try having a little family outing on or near the official "first day of spring" or other season. Go on a picnic or on some activity (depending on the time of year) and talk about the changes happening to the earth and about what family members will be doing during the season ahead.

Also if you try to have a weekly "family night" (see section on weekly traditions), you can make it even more fun by having a special seasonal dinner in the first week of the season.

With a family the size of ours, it's hard to find too many things to eat that everyone likes. But there are some, and at times in our family we've taken to having some of the more special "old standbys" on family nights. During the fall we would have some kind of fondue where the children could "dip and cook their own." In winter we would have some kind of warm soup or stew on family night. During the spring we'd have pasta, and during the summer we'd have salad.

On the first family night of each new season, we would have a special little ceremony welcoming the season and having something new related to the season for dinner.

—Linda

TRADITIONS OF SERVICE

VALUES
COMMUNICATION
EDUCATION
SENSITIVITY
RESPONSIBILITY

If things just aren't going well at your house, if you have a child who seems selfish and self-centered, or if your own burdens seem too hard to bear, there is one thing that is sure to help immediately, even though it may not totally solve all your problems. That thing is service.

We have good friends whose oldest son fell off the "deep end" into the drug scene. As is often the case, he was into drugs for two years before they suspected anything. By then it was too late. They tried everything from "tough love" to every imaginable drug rehabilitation facility—all without much success. "He had hair past his shoulders and had worn the same pair of jeans for a year," his mother said. "We were at a total loss as to what to try next."

Then an interesting thing happened. Somehow he met and connected with a mentally handicapped young man whom he somehow had a feeling he could help. He became totally occupied with thinking about how he could help this child, who was as lost as he was, only in a different way. Within a few months his parents saw this troubled youth change from "a druggy" to a loving, caring individual who was making enormous differences in someone else's life.

—Richard

Of course this is an extreme case, but we have found with our own children that service is a medicine for a wide variety of ills. Every time you take a meal to a sick friend or go out of your way to help someone in need, you are also helping your child, especially if he helps with the service process.

Even when there are no big problems, every trip to the homeless shelter to provide a dinner or play with the children there opens the eyes of our children to the immense needs of others as well as to their own blessings.

As mentioned, last summer we had a remarkable experience, as we had an opportunity to take our seven youngest children to work in an orphanage for fifty handicapped children in the Transylvanian Alps of Romania.

Our fourteen-year-old had centered his Eagle Scout project around gathering supplies for the orphanage from our generous neighborhood at home, and we truly looked like a Fourth of July parade when we boarded the plane with twenty-six bags stuffed with everything from a basketball hoop to a ride-on horse with wheels. Our first stop was Hungary, where we somehow managed to get all those bags to a hotel and back out to the airport by morning. The meal on the Romanian flight into Bucharest the next day was a panic. It consisted of four slabs of cold, nondescript meat, two unsalted and two too salty to eat, strangely textured goat cheese, coarse bread with strange flecks of stuff that resembled cardboard throughout, as well as a piece of black cake that proved inedible. The kids were looking at me with "uh-oh" eyes, and I was wondering how long our peanut butter and jelly and granola bars would last.

From Bucharest, in an old bus that registered 450,000 miles, we bumped along narrow, tree-lined roads into the Transylvanian Alps and the site of what we called our orphanage. We felt the scope of our challenge as we met our first group of children, who almost attacked us like bees drawn to honey when they saw our open arms. Each child in tattered clothes and mismatched shoes was starved for individual attention and begged to be held. With two children in my arms I looked down to see another biting firmly on the tongue of my tennis shoe, where he stayed anchored the whole time we were there that first afternoon.

Even though we couldn't communicate with one another verbally, we all felt an immediate bonding if at first only through sympathy. The children (ages three through ten) were squealing with delight and wetting all over us in their excitement. We were glad for all the expensive immunizations we'd had, even though we'd grumbled about it at the time.

Our days there were full of learning to love these little brothers and sisters through our darling little seventeen-year-old Romanian interpreter, who helped us teach little lessons from our Joy School material, designed for preschoolers, which was the mentality of most of the children there.

The headmistress thought the children could probably understand the lesson we had prepared on the Joy of the Body, but was doubtful about the lesson that we liked most, which is called the Joy of Confidence and Uniqueness. We were all delighted and quite amazed to see how much the children loved being placed in front of the room on a "throne" and told that they were unique. They each loved to see that the outline of their hand was different from that of everyone else.

Our children fell in love with so many of these little spirits in strange bodies. There was one special little girl, whom the kids named T.E. because she had been mangled at birth by someone who didn't know how to use forceps and abandoned, and her head was shaped like E.T.'s except that it

175

bulged out in opposite directions. She was so full of love and kindness and sensitivity that our children think that maybe someday they will feel privileged to call her "friend" in heaven.

We did survive quite nicely on bread and peanut butter and jelly as well as a very limited menu consisting of eggs, cucumber and tomato salad, vegetable soup, and pork steaks. Those who had been complaining about having to eat certain foods at home found that same "gross" food quite delightful upon our return. Plus I haven't heard one child say he or she doesn't have "anything to wear" since we got home. And even though they have been known to think they have the meanest parents in the world . . . they're exceptionally glad to have us!

—Linda

Whether it's a "big project" or simple small acts of service, helping others will do at least as much for our children as for those they help. And gradually the very idea of serving—of *contributing*—will become a habit.

We recently had the opportunity to attend a picnic for families of ambassadors from all over the world. It was quite a remarkable day, as our family was assigned to host the families from the Pakistan, Lesotho (a small nation surrounded by South Africa), and Bangladesh embassies.

Amazing stories surfaced as we spent time with these people. The Lesotho ambassador's brother-in-law had been killed three weeks earlier at a bus stop by rebels in South Africa. The ambassador for Pakistan had just returned from his homeland after having buried his wife, who had recently passed away. And the ambassador from Bangladesh said that things were stabilizing a little as far as famine went this year in his country.

I learned two very important things that day—first that people have problems no matter who they are or where they live, and second that good families have the same hopes and the same struggles all over the world.

The ambassador from Bangladesh asked, when he learned that our three older children were in Bulgaria, Romania, and England doing missionary work and humanitarian service, how we talked our children into doing such things.

My mind flashed back to family meetings we've had stressing the concept of "where much is given, much is expected," and the idea from one of my favorite songs, "Because I Have Been Given Much I Too Must Give." Children, especially when they are young, are so susceptible to suggestions! For so many years now we have had a little homemade sign on our refrigerator door that simply says, "Broaden and Contribute."

I guess the answer to the ambassador's question is that we've just been lucky so far, because after the good example of our older children, the others have just assumed that their lot in life is to give to others who need their help. We couldn't stop them if we tried, although we realize that each child will reach that family goal in his or her own way. Sometimes it's hard to really believe that our younger "whiners and wailers," who seem totally preoccupied with themselves, will at some point be able to help anyone, but it gives us hope to remember that the older children were just the same at that age.

—Linda

We don't tell these stories just to brag about our kids, but to remind you that raising a stronger family takes time, patience, and years of effort. The point is that you can make a difference—a dramatic difference—in your children's lives and in your family life. Kids do grow up and become worth bragging about. The hardest part is that the results often don't show up for some time—in many cases for years, when the children are older and out on their own in the real world. Ironically the most important results of building a strong family don't show up until the children grow up and physically leave the family.

THE TRADITION OF TRADITIONS

| COMMUNICATION |
| EDUCATION |
| INDIVIDUALITY |

Every family has traditions, and one important and fairly easy thing to do is to *recognize* and *formalize* those traditions a little so that family members are a bit more *aware* of them and able both to anticipate and to appreciate them more. This can be done just by writing down the traditions on a calendar—or, better yet, in your own "book" of family traditions.

It was late fall of the first year we lived in England. The Christmas season was approaching, and Thanksgiving, not celebrated in England of course, was almost upon us. We were trying to decide what to do for Thanksgiving and which Christmas traditions we wanted to keep (and which new English Christmas traditions we wanted to adopt).

I was walking past a very British stationery store one day and noticed a large, old-fashioned leather-bound "minute book" in the window. The idea hit me of cataloguing or writing down our young family's traditions and making a conscious effort to decide which traditions we valued most and wanted to continue with.

What a treasure that old minute book has become. It lists our family traditions by month. Each tradition has been "illustrated" in the book by one of the children. For example in January there are three traditions: On New Year's Day, while everyone is lying around recovering from the night before, we get out pictures and snapshots and any other memorabilia from the year just past and make up a scrapbook. Later in the month come Josh and Shawni's birthdays; the tradition there is to make a huge snowman in the front yard. And sometime during the month we stand each of the children up against the broom-closet door and mark their height to see how much they have grown during the year just passed.

Each of these three traditions is listed in the minute book under the heading "January." The scrapbook tradition is illustrated by seven-year-old Shawni (showing people with big smiles sitting at a table with lots of papers in front of a window full of snowflakes). The birthday tradition is illustrated by six-year-old Josh (showing a huge snowman with a carrot nose). The measuring tradition is illustrated by ten-year-old Eli (showing a big closet door with lots of marks and names on it and himself standing tall to be measured).

We've found that no matter how busy we get, two or three traditions per month, made "official" by their inclusion and illustration in the book, actually happen. The kids see to it that they do.

—Richard

3. Family Habits and Patterns—Monthly Traditions

When most people think of family traditions, the first thing that occurs to them is usually a holiday or birthday event. As great as these yearly traditions are, they actually have less impact on a family than the shorter-term family patterns or habits that should also be thought of as traditions.

To use the recipe metaphor again, you cook Thanksgiving dinner with all the trimmings once a year, but what nourishes your family during the rest of the year? What traditions can we serve up more often that teach values and the other principles as well as providing enjoyment and pulling everyone together?

Again remember that almost any good idea or activity can be turned into a tradition. As you read about some of the ones that we have used (or observed), be selective and choose those that appeal to you and that you think will work with and benefit your family.

Many people fill in new calendars at the start of each month. If you do, it is a good time to think about family and children and to schedule some traditions that ought to happen every month or so.

THE FIVE-FACET REVIEW

COMMUNICATION
MARRIAGE
SENSITIVITY
INDIVIDUALITY
GUIDANCE

One interesting thing about the "field" of parenting is that there really are no *experts*. There are psychiatrists and psy-

chologists and others who have studied child develop-
ment, but each child is an *individual,* different from any
other, and the only person with much chance of becoming
an expert on *that* child is that child's parent.

Often we know more about our own children than we
realize. It takes some focused thought and analysis to
make ourselves aware and use the things we already
"know." The five-facet review is a method for drawing out
and focusing on your child.

Once each month go out to dinner with your spouse (or
with someone else who knows your child if you are a
single parent), someplace private and quiet, and devote a
whole evening to a five-facet review of each of your children. Simply ask yourselves, "How is Jimmy doing *physically"* (growth, health, etc.)? "How is he doing *socially"*
(friends, etc.)? "How is he doing *mentally"* (in school,
etc.)? "How is he doing *emotionally"* (moods, attitudes,
etc.)? and "How is he doing *spiritually"* (values, responsibility, etc.)?

Take notes. Focus. Ask each other questions. Look for
any problems that may be emerging in any of the five
areas, but also look for opportunities—for aptitudes, for
emerging gifts, for things you should develop or give attention to. Don't worry about the complexity of trying to
think about five separate facets of each child. Generally
the review will help you to *simplify.* Most facets will be
fine, and you will usually come home having isolated two
or three "areas of concern" to focus on during the month
ahead.

We'll make two promises to parents who hold a five-
facet review once a month consistently over several
months: (a) You will avoid or curtail serious problems

because you will notice them early while they can still be "nipped in the bud"; and (b) you will *know* your children better as unique individuals, recognizing some of their special gifts and finding ways to help them develop themselves and become more appreciative of their own individuality.

Individual "Getaways"

COMMUNICATION
MARRIAGE
RESPONSIBILITY

While we're on the subject of things marriage partners can do together (i.e., the five-facet review), let's mention something that they should do *separately*, particularly if one spouse is taking most of the responsibility for staying home with the children.

Nothing is more difficult, complex, or emotionally demanding than being at home with growing children (people who have run large companies and also spent time at home raising children say there is no comparison). And most out-of-home jobs allow for *some* solitude and time alone, even if it just on the commute to and from work. For a parent staying home with children, anything even resembling solitude is hard to find.

If one of you is staying home, work together to give that person some individual getaway time.

While our children were young—while there were preschoolers in the home—Linda made the choice to stay home. Being a writer and a musician, she still found some professional opportunities, but she decided that "having it all" didn't necessarily mean "having it all at once."

She loved being with the children but, more than I realized, felt the pressure of being "on the job" twenty-four hours a day.

I remember coming home from a three-day business trip once early in our marriage and being so excited to see our two little preschoolers and only later in the evening noticing how tired Linda was and how frustrated she felt at having had no time for herself or to get anything personal accomplished. On an impulse I called a nice hotel close by and asked if they had a single room. I told Linda I thought I could handle the kids that night and the next day (Saturday). She took some correspondence, a book, and an overnight bag and went and spent twenty-four hours just taking care of herself.

She came back the next evening feeling like a new woman. I remember her saying how remarkable it seemed to set a pencil down, go into the bathroom, and come back and find the pencil still there.

Since then for us it has become something of a tradition to watch each other and encourage each other to take a short "alone" getaway once a month or so—maybe nothing more than a drive or a walk—to get some solitude.

—Richard

"DADDY DATES"
OR "MOMMY DATES"

VALUES
COMMUNICATION
EDUCATION
INDIVIDUALITY

Kids need individual time with a parent. Most good listening and good teaching takes place one-on-one. Yet most parents, busy as we are, find it hard to sit down and have a meal with our families, let alone spend individual time with a child.

We each look for our own ways. Some parents try to tuck a child in bed in the evening, having some time together there for a story or a little talk about the day. Some try to take an individual child on an errand to have some individual time in the car. But there are always so many other pressures and things to do, and the average parent, surveys show, ends up spending twelve minutes a *month* in individual contact with a child.

A tradition to combat this is a monthly "mommy date" or "daddy date." At the start of a month actually schedule an evening (or even a lunch hour) with a child and plan what you will do. (Make sure to let the child in on the planning.)

Enhance your child's experiences by *remembering* them through a *"mommy-date book."* This can be just a simple little notebook where each page is one date—almost like a small diary where the child *records* each date. If he's old enough to write, he might make an entry like "We went to lunch together at the Mexican restaurant. I had a fajita. Mom had a taco. On the way home we saw an ambulance and a fire engine at an accident on the freeway."

Even better than *writing* about the date is to bring something *from* the date that can be taped or stapled into the book that can help preserve the memory. A ticket, a piece of a program or menu, even a little piece of bark, *anything* from a place you visited is worth saving. Children, even years later, will be able to look at whatever you saved, stapled, or taped in the mommy-date book and remember the experience in surprising detail. What they will remember emotionally of course is a parent who loved them enough to take them places one-on-one.

One thing I looked forward to is going on an outing with my parents like going shopping, out to eat, or sometimes even going to some really special place that we both love to go to. My favorite one would probably be when we go to Basket Ball games.

When I was little we used to have a book called the Daddy date took (actually we still have it). We had to get one little souvineer when we went on a daddy date (like the wrapper from a straw, for example, if we went for a malt). One of my favorite ones was going to the zoo. I loved that. I brought home a little feather to tape in my daddy date book.

—Eli, 10

I have a little wierd book that has a lot of memories in it. I don't know how they all fit in there. Like in some of them it seems like I was just there but it was really four years ago. This book has in it a little souvineer from each place we would go on a daddy date. Like if we went to a movie we would bring back a ticket or something. These books are really cool. If I didn't have one I wouldn't remember half as much as I do with my dad.

These books are totally cool. I think you should have them in your family.

—Noah, 12

Me and dad or my mom we have wut we call dady and momy dat's. We go somewere speshl and tak smting from ther and put it in a book.

I love thos dady and momy dat's!

—Charity, 7

First-Sunday Family Testimonials

(WITH OPTIONAL FASTING)	COMMUNICATION
	SENSITIVITY
	INDIVIDUALITY
	GUIDANCE

We all know that it is healthy to express our feelings and important to communicate in our families about what we are thinking, experiencing, and feeling. But it is hard to start communication in a family unless we set aside a time and a place. Indeed communicating and expressing feelings once a month at some *scheduled* time will cause a big increase in the spontaneous, day-to-day communication that goes on.

For us the first Sunday of each month was the best time. Sunday is the most likely chance we have of getting everyone together for dinner, so we decided to meet on the first Sunday of each month in the living room before dinner and each stand for a moment to tell the rest of the family how we feel about each other and what we are grateful for.

The first few times we tried it, it was a little awkward, and some of the children didn't want to say anything (or to stand up and have everyone's attention focused on them). We didn't force them—just let those who wanted to stand and tell their feelings. Either Richard or I would go first, trying to talk simply and sincerely about our love for each child and about our appreciation for our home, our jobs, and other things we had been given.

We found that a remarkable *spirit* of peace and warmth seemed to come whenever a family member was expressing his love and feelings in this setting. Before long every child wanted to "take his turn" standing and saying how he felt.

We've tried one other thing that for us has made a difference. We've long been interested in *fasting* and in the enhanced feelings and sensitivity (not to mention gratitude) that seems to come from missing a couple of meals. We're also convinced that the body benefits from the digestive rest and cleansing that results from not eating for twenty-four hours. So we've tried not eating after lunch on the first Saturday of a month and then holding our family testimonial just before we have Sunday lunch together. We've invited the older children (over eight) to join us in the fast. It *deepens* the participant's spirit of appreciation and love and adds a greater sense of calm and peace to this monthly family meeting. And it allows parents to teach valuable lessons about self-discipline, shared purpose, and consumption as well as gratitude.

—Linda

3. (cont.) Family Habits and Patterns—Weekly or Sunday Traditions

Beyond the yearly and monthly traditions you try to develop in your family, you may want to add some weekly habits or patterns. Again don't try to adopt too many of these regular practices or weekly commitments at once. Just pick (or adapt) the ones that your family will enjoy.

Many of the following ideas are suggested for *Sunday.* This is because, for many families, Sunday is either a day of religious observance or at least a day on which there is still freedom or flexibility in their schedule. Obviously if another day is better for you, these ideas will work equally well on another day.

Sunday Awards

VALUES
COMMUNICATION
INDIVIDUALITY

Sitting down together as a family for a meal simply isn't easy these days. But Sunday is often the best opportunity. During Sunday dinner present some simple "awards" that recognize your children's value-based behavior. The awards need be nothing more complicated than some hand-drawn letters mounted on a piece of construction paper. For instance:

LFR = Leader for the Right
SS = Self-starter (did things without being reminded)
HUP = Honesty Under Pressure
GR = Good Reader
NAP = Neat as a Pin
HE = Hungry Eater

Design awards that represent qualities or behavior that your children need help on or that you want to focus attention on.

At dinner ask, "Who's in the running for the Leader for the Right award?" Have the kids try to think of anytime during the past week where they set a good example or made a good decision or read some extra books—whatever's needed in your family. A child who comes up with a good example gets the "award" pinned on his door during the week ahead. Use these regular awards as an opportunity to explain and reinforce good behavior in your children.

One day when I was in sixth grade (I am now in the 7th grade) there was a foreign boy from Korea. People had been mean to

188

him a lot, mainly because he was heavy and I guess also because he was different. I always was able to look back and remember that our family talked about being a leader for the right a lot so I was always able to go put my arm around him and try to help him out and he always told me thanks for talking to him and helping him out.

Anyway, this one day at school, it was the winter and he sliped on some ice and fell. For some reason the kids around him started laughing at him and they kicked him while he was on the ground. I just kind of went nuts when I saw this happening. I said to a couple of friends, "Come on guys, let's go help him." So me and them went and moved people away and helped him up and then we went inside with him to be sure he was O.K.

—Noah, 12

Sunday Awards is a tradition that clearly enhances values and that kids like because it gives recognition, praise, and attention. It's a good example of a family practice that isn't tied to a birthday or an anniversary or more familiar traditions but that can play an invaluable role in building a stronger family.

SUNDAY SESSIONS

COMMUNICATION
RESPONSIBILITY
SENSITIVITY

One of the subtle but important societal changes of the last twenty years is how differently Americans view and live the seventh day of the week. Sunday has been transformed from being a day when people stayed at home or went to church and stores were closed to being the primary recreation day, the setting for major sports events, a time to travel and play.

One of the problems with this transformation is that people don't do the kind of thinking, reassessing, or planning for the week ahead that used to happen more on the stay-at-home or go-to-church Sundays.

The ancient concept of the sabbatical—a one-in-seven day or period in which to evaluate, meditate, and re-create—was a sound idea. Weekly planning is very different from daily scheduling or "day-timing." It is longer range, more conceptual, less pressured. People who spend a little time once a week *examining* their lives and where they're going seem to have a clearer perspective and to go about the rest of the week with more calmness as well as more purpose.

One good tradition to try with your family is to have each member take an hour each Sunday to sit, alone and quiet, for a Sunday Session. They should think about the week just passed and set some goals for the week ahead in three areas: family, work, and self. For example ask yourself what you can do during the coming week for your family, for your work, and for yourself. You'll find that these weekly goals will be "choose-to-dos" rather than the "have-to-dos" of daily planning.

We had tried to follow the tradition of Sunday Sessions early in our marriage, and when Saren, age five and in kindergarten, wanted to know what we were doing, I said we were setting goals. Predictably she wanted to know what goals were and if she could have some.

Without thinking too hard about it, I said, "Well, you have

to write them—so maybe when you can write." Saren said, "Can't I draw goals?"

I thought about that . . . and handed her a paper and pencil. "Goals are the things you want to do. Draw one thing you want to do at school this week and one thing you want to do for someone in your family this week."

I'll never forget Saren's first Sunday Session. It was a little picture of two stick figures holding hands and another of a big figure handing something to a smaller figure. Saren explained, "The first one is me, and this is a new friend I'm going to make at school this week because I need a new friend." The second picture she said was "me sharing my new doll with Shawni."

It led to a little discussion of why she needed a new friend (another friend had been mean to her the week before) and of how much little sister Shawni liked it when she played dolls with her.

I learned that day that children can learn to set goals even before they learn to write and that talking about a child's goal can tell you things about them that you wouldn't know enough to ask about.

At this point Sunday Sessions became a family tradition.

—Richard

Children can also set longer-range goals, as illustrated by this statement from Noah:

Each person in our family has what we call our Eyrealm books. In our Eyrealm books we make long term goals.

Some of my long term goals are: Get maried and have a family, finish college, etc. Some of my short term goals are:

Get good grades in school this year, be a leader for the rite, etc.

I think that all goals can help everyone a lot in life. And in many ways.

Even though sometimes I get cought up in my every day thing I think that it is good to know what my goals are so that I can work toward them along the way.

On Sundays we try (Dad says we do it all the time but we don't) to have something called Sunday Sessions. This is when we look at our Eyrealm books.

—*Noah, 12*

Sunday Partnership Meetings

| COMMUNICATION |
| MARRIAGE |
| SENSITIVITY |

Of course one of the most important things married parents can do for their children and their family is to take good care of their relationship with each other. The old addage "The best thing a father can do for his children is to love their mother" is absolutely true.

There are some other familiar sayings about marriage, however, that are pretty unrealistic. One says, "Never let the sun set on a disagreement," or "Resolve everything between you before you go to sleep." Most couples who have tried to live by these find that there are some long, sleepless nights and that sometimes the sun *rises* on a still-present disagreement.

Other guidelines, some say, are more realistic: "Agree to disagree" on certain things, or "Some things are better left unsaid."

But still another saying worries us: "Unexpressed feelings never die, they just get buried and come forth later in uglier forms."

So how does a married couple get things sorted out and clear the air frequently and regularly without staying up all night?

One possibility is another good habit or tradition to try on Sundays (although, again, this can be scheduled for any day that's convenient for you). Have a short meeting to coordinate your schedules for the week ahead and to talk about some individual and collective goals. Then each take a moment to express feelings—one talking, the other listening—then switch. In this kind of a setting you'll find it less awkward to talk of positive feelings, to express your love and appreciation, and to compliment your spouse. Then, in an atmosphere of love and trust, express anything that bothers you, that is on your mind or feels unresolved. In that setting it's easier than usual to really communicate, and harder than usual to offend.

With this tradition, in addition to better communication and a greater feeling of partnership, you will ensure that disagreements, bad feelings, or lapses in trust don't linger for more than a few days or begin to grow and fester.

WEEKLY DATE | COMMUNICATION
| MARRIAGE

As divorce rates grow and marriage seems for so many to represent less and less of a commitment (and as we all get busier and seem to have less and less time), there is great need for traditions and habits that improve and protect communication and preserve excitement and romance between marriage partners.

The same *kinds* of things that helped you to fall in love can help you to stay in love. Courtship doesn't have to end at marriage.

Start a tradition of choosing one night of the week for a date. Go out, just the two of you; do things you like to do together; and *talk*. Try not to schedule anything else or let other things interfere, and when something unavoidable does come up, reschedule your date to another night.

Back when we were newlyweds and graduate students, we attended a church where, one Sunday, a respected religious leader got us to make a commitment we've tried to keep ever since.

This man, from the podium, in the midst of a sermon he was giving, suddenly said that he'd decided to take his wife out on a date once a week and felt that it was such a good idea that he wondered who among the married people in the congregation would make the same commitment—by a show of hands. Then he just stood there, silently, with his hand raised high, and waited for us to raise our hands.

After what seemed like five minutes of gradual hand raising (the pressure built as those who had raised their hands looked around at those who hadn't), almost everyone signified that they would.

We don't know how many kept the commitment, but we expect that those who did have fared better in marriage than those who didn't.

—Richard

194

FAMILY NIGHT

COMMUNICATION
EDUCATION
INDIVIDUALITY

Family time—real family time, when people talk and play together—is harder and harder to find. For most families, just getting everyone in the same house at the same time is difficult. The fact that it is difficult is the *reason* that a tradition of a weekly family night is so critically important.

Pick the night of the week when family members are the least committed to outside activities and obligations and designate it as family night. Explain to the kids that it's a time for family *activities* and family talk.

Think ahead enough to have something interesting and appealing to do each family night. Depending on what you and your kids enjoy, and on your budget, look for good activities. Sometimes it might be a movie or physical activity or ball game, other times it might just be a game or a video at home.

Try hard not to schedule or commit to anything else on family night—and ask the kids to do the same. Things will come up, but hold family night (on the night you've designated) whenever you can.

Communication will happen naturally on family night if you're having fun together. But don't make communication the goal. Don't say, "Okay, it's family night, let's talk," or "Tell me everything that's on your mind," or "Let's have an interview." Instead let the goal be to have *fun* and to be together. When you are enjoying yourself and each other, communication will just happen.

THE "B.F." PROGRAM

VALUES
RESPONSIBILITY
INDIVIDUALITY
GUIDANCE

Benjamin Franklin had a marvelous personal tradition designed to help him improve his own character and values. He selected certain words, such as *punctuality* or *candor*, that described character traits he desired, and concentrated on them one at a time.

We sometimes forget that we become better parents not by changing our kids but by changing ourselves. Try making up your own list of one-word character traits that would make you a better parent or a better spouse. Go through your list mentally every other day or as you do something routine (shave, shower, run, exercise, drive to work, etc.). As you think about each word, think about times when it *has* described you, when you *have* behaved as though you had that trait—and recommit yourself to it.

Years ago I decided I had to start jogging a couple of times a week if I was going to stay in any semblance of shape. The trouble was jogging was so boring. Then I came across the BF idea. I thought of certain "wannabe" words—things I wished described me as a father ("consistent," "confident," "calm") or as a husband ("patient," "partner"), or as a person ("serendipity," "stewardship"), and started reciting these words mentally and thinking about them as I jogged. It made the exercise less boring, and focused my mind a little more often on what I wanted to become.

—Richard

CHURCH ACTIVITY

VALUES
EDUCATION
MARRIAGE
RESPONSIBILITY
SENSITIVITY
GUIDANCE

Though it may not be a weekly tradition for everyone, attending a church or place of worship on Sundays (or Saturdays, as the case may be) benefits virtually everyone who does it. And as a *family* tradition there is nothing that can bind and bond (and provide an opportunity to discuss values) more effectively than attending a church or synagogue of your choice.

There are many people who (often with some justification) resent and resist all "organized religion," but by not affiliating, not going to or even *looking* for a church or synagogue or even discussion group that they can be comfortable with and learn and benefit from, they end up depriving themselves of a valuable opportunity for communication, for learning new things, for focusing their thinking. In the family context participation in church activities can provide valuable support, a sounding board, or just a peaceful moment in a chaotic week.

Back when I lived at home, getting up for church on Sunday mornings was one of my hardest things. I started wondering why God made Sundays right after Saturday nights—when you'd been out late and needed sleep.

Still, we went as a family, so it was hard not to go.

Now, here at college, I'm so glad I have the habit of going to church on Sundays. With the pressure of my classes and other things it's so nice to have Sunday as a change of pace—to know I'm going to have time to think and plan and be at church.

—Saydi, 18

3. (cont.) Family Habits and Patterns— Daily Family Traditions

Remember that you'll already have several daily or weekly family traditions as you implement the *family economy* (pegboard, payday, etc.) and the *family legal system* (keeping a room or "zone" clean, the "repenting bench," etc.). In addition to these, and to other habits or patterns you already have, you may want to try some of the following ideas. Experiment with some of them. See which ones work in your family. As noted elsewhere, don't try to do too much or too many.

DINNER TOGETHER	COMMUNICATION
	EDUCATION
	SENSITIVITY
	INDIVIDUALITY

There was a time when the family dinner table was the place to communicate and educate. There was even something called the dinner hour, which implied that families actually sat around a table for an hour and talked to each other. Now most households use the cupboard or kitchen bar more than the table, and eating is more like random refueling than dining. Some have said (with their tongues only partially in their cheeks) that the real culprit in the decline of family communication is fast food.

A quite remarkable survey and article appeared in *USA Today* in October 1993—as we were writing this book. It was an attempt to determine cause and effect regarding high-achieving, well-adjusted adolescents. Essentially they took a large sample of kids who did well in school and other activities and who enjoyed a high level of self-esteem, and they tried to determine what behavioral patterns or other tendencies matched up. In other words was there something these "successful" kids all did, some common ingredient or factor that was present in all of their lives and therefore could be viewed as a cause? They looked at economic factors (were most of them in a certain socioeconomic class?), at religious factors (did most of them go to church?), and dozens more. The single thing that correlated most directly with solid achievement and strong self-image was sitting down and eating dinner together on a regular basis with their parents.

—Linda

Most families make some effort to sit down and eat together—depending on the ages of their children, work schedules, and a host of other things. Some families do well to have a meal together once a week, perhaps on Sundays; others actually eat together most evenings. In any case, given the possible rewards, it's worth the effort to institute a regular dinnertime in your family.

DINNERTIME VERBAL GAMES

| EDUCATION |
| COMMUNICATION |
| INDIVIDUALITY |

As good a tradition as "dinner together" is, it can be made even better by playing some entertaining and educational verbal games together around the dinner table. Following are some constructive ones that can be adapted to children of different ages:

THE QUESTION GAME. One problem with most public schools is that only the "right answer" is rewarded. Children are rarely encouraged or taught how to ask good questions and are seldom praised for their questions. In the question game a parent names a subject and each family member thinks of the most interesting or hardest question he can ask about that topic. Amazingly children who think of a question that no one can answer can sometimes be seen voluntarily pulling out an encyclopedia *to look* for the answer.

One night in question game Dad said, "a baseball." I started to ask something about the game because I know a lot of statistics. But Dad said, "No, about the ball *itself." So I asked what a baseball was made out of. Dad's answer was leather and string—not such a good answer. So after dinner I was curious so I wanted to do something really weird. I wanted to look it up in an encyclopedia.*

—Eli, 10

SPEECHES. Each family member stands and speaks for sixty seconds on an extemporaneous subject. The idea is to make it as dramatic, interesting, and individualistic as you can. A parent might say, "Jimmy, speak for sixty seconds on *doorknobs*." Jimmy might talk about their shape or variety, or about how they work mechanically, or about what life would be like without them. He might make up a song about doorknobs or give several doorknobs in the house a name. The idea is to learn to think (and speak) on your feet. Many kids (and many parents) will be a bit awkward at first, but as you make it fun and give encouragement, everyone will improve dramatically.

This can be a terrific confidence builder in young children, and will lead to their being more comfortable with public speaking later on.

In our family, topics went from things like "doorknobs" to "why we eat vegetables" or "things I could have done when Billy hit me that would have been better than hitting him back," or "the saddest and happiest moments of my day." We found we were using "speeches" not only to increase verbal and thinking skills but to get subjects that needed communication discussed and to let children tell us the very things that we would otherwise lecture them about. (It is amazing that kids usually know what they should do or what they need correcting on—long before we tell them.)

—Linda

"PINK STINKS." Question: "What is a crimson sleeping place?" Answer: "A red bed." This is a contagious little verbal game that helps children learn to rhyme and to think of alternate ways of phrasing things. (Question: "What is a cowardly guy?" Answer: "A yellow fellow.")

(Question: "What is a pasta sword?" Answer: "A spaghetti machete.")

THE WHAT'S SIMILAR? GAME. Say, "What is similar about a turtle and a telephone?" or any pair of apparently dissimilar objects. Kids are used to logical-connection, one-correct-answer questions at school, and this game helps them think in less conforming, more creative ways.

"Telephone and turtle" happened to be the subjects the first time we played this game at our dinner table. The older, school kids couldn't think of anything similar about them. One of the preschoolers said, "Well, they're both kind of curvy." The school kids wanted to know if that was "the right answer." When we said there were lots more right answers, they started thinking in a different way. We got answers like "They both don't eat at McDonald's," and from an older child, "If held under water long enough, they'd both cease to function."
—Richard

JOURNALS, LETTERS, READING ALOUD, AND POETRY

VALUES
COMMUNICATION
EDUCATION
SENSITIVITY
INDIVIDUALITY

Children learn less and less about writing in schools. Being able to write clearly and expressively helps a person to think and speak more clearly. And journals, letters, and poetry preserve a record of our ideas, our thoughts, and our experiences.

Buy each child a nice journal or diary and talk about the benefits of the habit or tradition of writing a little each night or at least a couple of times a week.

We were fortunate to have an eldest daughter who took to journal writing and who named each journal. Her first one was called "Esmarelda" and she started each entry with "Dear Esmarelda." Something about writing to Esmarelda made her entries almost like letters to a real person. Now, as a graduate student, she's on her tenth or eleventh journal, each with a different name, each representing a different year of her life. Her younger brothers and sisters, intrigued by the names, got their own journals, named them, and followed suit.

—Linda

Get children corresponding regularly with someone—a friend, a cousin, an older brother or sister who has moved away. Encourage them to keep copies of some of their letters—perhaps to put them into their journal.

Just as we wrote this page of the book, Noah was writing a letter to his Grandma Jacobson who, at age eighty-seven, is still a great sports fan and has long talks with the kids about the NBA and the basketball standings. We asked Noah if we could include his letter.

October 11, 1993
McLean, Virginia

Dear Grandma J,
How are you? I am doing pretty good. I am meeting new friends and I am fiting in pretty good.

203

It is so green here. And now the trees leaves are changing to different colors like red, orange, and yellow. are the leaves changing yet in Idaho?

How is Mrs. Trusel? Are you still doing such good work at the geneology place and do you still go to play the piano for people over at the nursing home?

To go to school I have to wake up at 6:20 a.m. It is hard to wake up. School is harder here than in the west. I am keeping up with the work though.

Every day I meet more people if I possibly can. I also ran for vice president at my school but I lost. It's O.K. though because I learned a lot and met a lot of new kids.

I can't wait until we see you again. When are you coming to visit? I also can't wait to go to Bear Lake next summer and waterski.

I miss you so much but I guess that I will be out there again before I know it.

I love you!!!!!

Noah Eyre

P.S. Do you want the Braves to win it? I do! I can't wait until the NBA starts again. I think they will be great this year!

When our second daughter started her first year at Boston University, we went with her to freshman orientation. The university president, addressing both parents and new students, said, "Write more letters and make fewer phone calls. Then, at the end of the year, instead of a stack of expensive phone bills you'll have a stack of priceless treasures."

—Richard

Reading aloud is a wonderful family tradition, one that used to be common and is now very rare. Reading *with* family members not only enhances reading skills and helps build children's imaginations, it creates a warm feeling of unity and shared, intimate experiences within a family.

We had never read aloud in our family—except for the occasional bedtime story to a small child—until one summer when we spent our vacation camping in the wilderness of eastern Oregon where there was no electricity (and therefore no TV or music). We had brought along two books: *Black Beauty* and *The Secret Garden*. In the evenings there was nothing to do but read by the light of the Coleman lantern. Even though initially the older children scoffed at a "children's book" like *The Secret Garden* and they balked some at reading a "horse story," each child became hooked within the first hour of reading. Often a child would sneak off with the book to read it in their tents with a flashlight until three A.M. Several nights we read until the wee hours. We felt lifted, united, often inspired.

—Linda

One of my favorite traditions is reading books out loud together. You wouldn't think this would be as fun as it is. You can actually see more in your mind than you could on T.V.

We do it most when we're on a trip or away from the busy schedule. I think it started one time years ago when my mom read us a book called The Education of Little Tree—*a book about a small Indian boy in his own words. When she first started reading, people were a little restless (we were used to T.V.) but once we got into it we wouldn't let her stop reading.*

—Talmadge, 14

Poetry is a particularly expressive and revealing form of writing. Children, especially if they start early, are natural poets and can produce some delightful poetry as well as short stories.

If you get any kind of a read-aloud tradition going, occasionally read some interesting and dramatic poetry or some short stories rather than long books. Then, on a trip or a long Sunday afternoon, encourage family members to try their best at *writing* a poem or a story to be shared with other family members.

Three Daily Priorities

| MARRIAGE |
| RESPONSIBILITY |
| GUIDANCE |

A Gallup Poll showed that, when asked for their most difficult personal challenge, more Americans named "finding balance" (between work, family, and personal needs) than any other concern. Often work takes so much time and energy that there is little of either left for family or for personal needs, and we are left feeling guilty or unfulfilled or both.

But balance is not really a question of giving "equal time" to each facet of life. It's a question of doing *something* (even a little thing) *each* day for each priority.

Try this tradition. Before making your daily list of have-to-do's, write down *one* thing you will do that day for a family member and *one* thing you will do for yourself. Even if they are small things—play catch with Billy, exercise for ten minutes, compliment Sally on her math-test grade, take a five-minute rest—just doing one little "choose-to-do" each day for family and for self will help you keep a sense of balance.

This habit can become the kind of pattern or tradition that keeps you, as a parent, more constantly aware of the needs of your family and your children. It can also create in you a balance and a sense of peace that will increase your patience with your children.

A Secret Service

VALUES
RESPONSIBILITY
SENSITIVITY

Traditions or habits that involve service are of particular value because in addition to helping other people they increase the sensitivity and love that is *in* our children and help kids to be less selfish.

Service becomes more fun and more appealing to kids when it is kept secret. Start this tradition on a Sunday by putting each family member's name in a hat and then each drawing a name. Each family member keeps the name he's drawn a secret and tries to do little anonymous "good deeds" for that person during the week (anything from making their bed to leaving them a little note). On the next Sunday see who can guess who their benefactor was— then reveal who was each person's secret buddy.

We have somethig cald secrit budys. We put names in a hat and then we shak it and pick one. that prsin is speshel! Then you do somethig nise to them. Last time I frgot my secrit budy. He was sad but, at list I did not have to do anything that wek. Wen I do do sum secrit servis, I fell so so so good to.

207

Ones I was a secrit budy to Saydi. I gave her huggs and huggs. And ones she was my secrit budy and she decoradid my room. I new it was her! But sill it was a surpris! I love to do somethig speshl to a nother prsin.

—Charity, 7

Once you've done secret buddies in your family a few times, encourage children to do some anonymous kind deeds for others (schoolmates, friends, teachers, etc.). You'll find that starting this tradition can help you teach your children the value of generosity, a value they'll share and spread for the rest of their lives.

All of my life I have witnessed how effective anonymous service is. I've always wondered who benefits more from it, the person giving or the one receiving. Helping others causes you to look outside yourself and saves you from drowning in self pity. When I was a high school sophomore my older sister pointed out to me how foolish kids were at my age because all they thought about was themselves. I realized that that was the biggest problem I had.

A couple of my friends and I decided to try service in order to make ourselves happier. We had noticed some really shy and sad kids at our school, ones who most people disregarded as the nerds and who were rarely involved and treated nicely. We picked two in particular, a boy and a girl, both of whom were very poor. We first made some efforts to talk to and befriend but that wasn't enough so, since it was nearing Christmas, we decided to buy them Christmas gifts and anonymously deliver them with a note of appreciation and compliments. It was a small gesture on our part.

About ten of us all donated a little money and we went shopping and bought some really nice gifts, wrapped them up and on Christmas day we all piled in our old van and drove across the city to scout out their homes. My dad disguised himself in an old leather jacket and sun glasses and delivered the gifts while we sat ducked down in the car enjoying the surprised and excited expressions.

Those happy surprised smiles and the joy that filled their faces at school the next week were the best Christmas gift I have ever received.

—Saydi, 18

THREE-WAY PARTNERSHIP	COMMUNICATION
	MARRIAGE
	GUIDANCE

Raising children is an important and difficult business—important and difficult enough that parents need all the help they can get.

To those who believe in God or a higher power, it is logical to believe that this power also deems the welfare of children to be important—important enough to give insight or guidance to parents who ask for it.

Children are complex and have needs beyond the comprehension of even the most observant and analytical parent. Those who believe in God (it is interesting that so many who do call him Father) generally believe that he knows our children better than we do.

It is extremely helpful to think of child rearing as a partnership enterprise—a partnership between earthly and heavenly parents wherein the former can seek and receive help from the latter.

We, like most parents, pray for and about our children. In our case we try to pray together at night before going to bed. The usual pattern is that one or the other of us says the prayer out loud—a spontaneous one, in our own words.

One night several years ago Linda prayed and left out a couple of things I was worried about, so I said an additional prayer. She said she learned some things about what was on my mind by what I said in my prayer and why didn't we each pray in turn each night.

This has evolved to where one of us starts the prayer and, when finished, instead of closing, squeezes the other's hand and the other continues the same prayer and then closes.

It has given us the feeling of a three-way partnership. The two of us, praying together to a "managing partner" who can help us to go beyond our own capacities.

—Richard

For those to whom prayer has less appeal, meditation and quiet, sober contemplation (both individually and as a couple), as well as spoken, spontaneous sharing of their concerns can have some of the same result.

I had the privilege of hearing Mrs. Norman Vincent Peale speak at an American Mothers Convention at the Waldorf-Astoria, in New York, when our children were young. Much of what she said is now forgotten, but one example she gave has become a part of the fabric of our household.

She said that when her children were small, she (and her husband when he was there) had a brief meeting with them just before they left for school. They read a short passage of inspiration together—sometimes just one verse from the Bible. Next they talked together about their challenges for the day. Sometimes the child had a test or a parent had an important presentation. A family prayer ended this ten-minute meeting that specifically asked for help for each person with a special need.

She said that sometimes they even synchronized their watches so that at the time a child was due to give a talk in a class or take a test, they could each say a prayer for the other at that very moment. After picking this up and doing it in our family, even our children who are living overseas or at college know that they are getting a little extra help from home as they mention in their letters specific dates and times of events important in their lives. There is not a better way to bring family unity and help kids feel that they are involved with and in tune with and helping each other.

—Linda

READING AND MEMORIZING | VALUES
| GUIDANCE

"What we put into the mind is as important as what we put into the body." "The spirit, like the body, needs constant nourishment." Phrases like these were heard more a generation ago than they are now, but they are equally true today.

A phrase we do hear today—usually with reference to computers but equally applicable to humans, and to *minds*—is "Garbage in, garbage out." Our children today ingest so much mental garbage, from television and other sources, that they need, more than ever, some mental *nourishment*, some clear thinking, some *wisdom*, some mental moorings that will help them live up to their values and see their lives in proper perspective.

211

Sometimes all it takes to make a right decision or react well in a situation is to remember a story, experience, or phrase that gives courage or reminds you of something good or right.

One day when I was at the NBA all-star weekend which was held in our city last year, I was walking through and looking at the exibits. By quinsedance we saw a sign that said SLAM DUNK contest—so we walked down to where it was and went to sign up. I went to my dad and said "Dad it is okay I don't want to do it" but he told me what have I got to loose. I thought I have nothing to loose so we went in, sat down in the stands until they called us down. I was still so scared but my brother said remember the saying we learned, "Our doubts are traders and make us loose the good we oft might win by failing to attempt." So I said okay I'll go down. So I went down and I finally was not very scared any more. So I went down and won the slamdunk contest. I was stunned I had won because there were about 60 boys entered. After that they told me that I was to go back the next night and play in a championship so in the end I was very happy because I got a special book and a whole box of basketball cards.
—Eli, 10

Memorizing short quotations or verses, reading aloud from good literature or Scripture—these are great family traditions. But time is short, kids are busy and more interested in "exciting" things, and it's hard to find a quiet, serious time for this sort of thing. Yet some families do it. Following are some alternate ways some families have experimented with:

- Just have one short saying (or Scripture) that you post on the refrigerator each week. Any family member who learns it by Saturday gets extra points or a bonus on "payday" (see the family-economy section).
- Find time to read aloud to smaller children once or twice a week as they go to bed. If the choice is between turning the light off and going to sleep or listening to something, most kids will listen, even if what you're reading them is classic literature.
- Read aloud on camping trips, or while traveling, or anywhere else you find yourself where there are fewer than normal distractions.
- Read a paragraph or a great quotation or two before eating whenever you are able to get everyone together for a meal.
- If you try to have family prayer (and there is *no* better tradition than this), read together briefly before having the prayer.
- Ask children to find sayings or phrases that they like and want to memorize, and learn them together.

SAYING "I LOVE YOU"

| COMMUNICATION |
| MARRIAGE |
| SENSITIVITY |

I never thought of saying "I love you" as a tradition until one day when I dropped a child off at school when I had a friend in the car. This teenager had forgotten an assignment and had driven home from school to get it, only to run out of gas. She was fussing all the way back to the school about being late for the next class. She jumped out of the car and flung back the familiar words, " 'Bye. I love you."

"How sweet," said my friend, "that she remembered to say I love you even though she was so distraught." I hadn't really realized before then that even though it is sweet, it was mostly a habit or a tradition. For as long as I can remember, we have all been saying " 'Bye, I love you," every time anybody left the house, got out of the car, or signed off on the phone. It's a nice tradition even though it is sometimes said by rote without much thought. We always mean it.

Now, since our children have left home for faraway places like Romania, Bulgaria, England, and Boston, it has been a tradition to think of wild ways we love each other. One child will write, "I love you all up to the moon," and the next one will write, "I love you all the way up to Mars and back around the earth three hundred times." Silly, but kind of a visual way to remind ourselves of how much we love and miss one another.

—Linda

By-Product of the Three Steps: A Better Marriage

(or, for a single parent, better relationships and better teamwork with others who love and care for your child)

As we were writing this book, we found a message on our answering machine from *USA Today* asking for a comment on a new movie, *Mrs. Doubtfire,* starring Robin Williams and Sally Field. It made some social statements about families and divorce, the reporter said, and would we call her in the morning with a comment for an article.

We hadn't seen the movie, so we went that night. The basic story, for anyone who didn't see it (which may be no one by now—the movie has done so well), is about two people who had drifted apart but both passionately loved their three children. The mother gets custody and the dad, desperate to be with his kids, disguises himself as a matronly woman and gets hired by the mom as the housekeeper.

He is eventually found out, but the mother, pleased with how well everything has gone for the kids, allows him to keep coming every day, as himself, to care for the kids after school before she gets home from work. The divorce goes forward. The movie ends with a monologue about how some moms and dads get divorced but it doesn't matter so long as they both love their kids.

Two days later *USA Today* quoted me saying that the movie had a hopeful, consoling message for kids caught in a divorce or separation but a terrible message for parents who were having problems and were tempted to throw in the towel too soon.

Robin Williams and Sally Field's marriage didn't look that bad on the screen. They were both appealing, caring people. They had some personality conflicts and were not communicating their needs or feelings to each other, but the situation didn't seem hopeless. We worried that couples might see it and think, "Our marriage is way worse than theirs—and divorce worked for them—let's do it."

The movie showed no real effort on the part of the parents to reconcile or to communicate about what was wrong, nor any of the trauma involved for children. It was well done, funny, and appealing and thus, like so much of what gets conveyed via our media today, insidious in that it made a wrong choice look so good.

—Richard

Contrary to a lot of well-publicized but misinterpreted* statistics, only 10 percent of all ever-married men and 13 percent of ever-married women have *ever* been divorced. This in turn means that almost 90 percent of all marriages survive (Louis Harris, *Inside America*, 1987). Of these American adults who are not married (including those

---

* Since there have sometimes been half as many divorces as marriages in a given year some have concluded that half of all marriages will end in divorce. This is a misinterpretation of statistics. Since there are far more married adults than single adults, a far smaller percentage of married people are getting divorced than the much higher percentage of single adults who are getting married.

widowed or divorced), 80 percent plan on wedlock in the future. Over 90 percent of children spend all or most of their childhood in a home with two married parents.

Of course there are some marriages that should be ended and some situations in which there is such stress and even abuse that the children are better off with just one parent. But we should all understand and appreciate the odds. We now have thirty or forty years' worth of very conclusive statistics that show that children from two-parent homes (none of which are *perfect* marriages) are at substantially less risk for drug abuse, teen pregnancy, school dropout, suicide, and a whole host of other problems. Statistically they have a better chance of being good students, of feeling well adjusted socially, and of being happy.

Too many divorces are justified (or rationalized) with the old line about not wanting children to have to continue to be exposed to the tension of a bad relationship. We forget that what children *really need* to be exposed to is parents trying and working *hard* to save something that is deeply important. Nothing manifests a parent's love for a child more than struggling to keep that child's family together. As mentioned earlier, the old cliché is true, "The best thing a father or mother can do for a child is to love that child's mother or father."

Nothing is better for a relationship than working together on a common goal . . . or hope . . . or project. Our children are our hope. Their happiness should be our most important goal. And they are certainly a *project*. In our world, with dual careers, varying interests, and limitless options, married couples often find that they have less and less in common in their day-to-day lives. What they do have in common is their children. If they can talk about those children, really communicate about their needs, their gifts, their progress, and their problems, they will not only become capable, nurturing parents, they will strengthen their marriage.

If this section of the book is to have meaning, we have to be candid about our own marriage and how far it has been from smooth and easy. It's both funny and completely deceptive when we go out and speak or lecture on parenting and families and someone comes up afterward and says, "Well, it's easy for you two—you're so obviously happily married and you agree on everything."

That's just not true. If there was ever a courtship or a marriage built on conflict, it is ours. We are both so strong-willed that it's pathetic. We couldn't even agree in the first weeks of our marriage on the right kind of Christmas tree or how it should be decorated.

Somewhere, though, maybe through luck, we did decide that children were worth the struggle to get it together and that, in terms of their welfare and what we wanted to teach them and give to them, we would work as hard as it took to agree and to reconcile our differences.

Over the years the children have been our greatest bond. Through them and our devotion to them we have strengthened and built our love for each other.

—Linda

Even if you try, even if there is some real effort put into communication, it's not easy for married parents to be in agreement about what children need. Perhaps you and your spouse were raised very differently from each other.

218

Perhaps you are part of a stepfamily or a blended family and thus have a more complicated range of physical and emotional relationships with your children. Perhaps one of you is very involved as a parent and the other not very involved at all. How do you get it together? How do you come together?

The great thing about the three steps is that they are *simple.* Not easy, but conceptually simple. Just three basic things to work on, to sort out, to communicate about and implement together. Many parents, intimidated by involved psychological techniques, have looked at these three steps and said, "I can do that."

You can set up some basic rules. You can establish a simple family economy. You can refine and get more out of your family traditions. And you can think and talk about each of the three steps together and learn about each other as you go.

Single parents can do the same *kind* of thing with someone else who loves and cares for their children—a grandparent, an aunt or uncle, a neighbor or friend, a teacher or sitter. Have a five-facet review with the next-closest adult to your children—whoever that is. If you are divorced or separated and share custody or have visitation, consider getting together for a five-facet review or a discussion of the three steps and what you could each do to implement them.

The important thing of course, to all of us, is the children. When we think hard and work hard for their welfare with the three steps or with anything else, the by-product may well be the improved quality of our own relationships.

Postlude

As you've probably noticed, we've managed to present most of the key ideas in this book in *threes*. And, not surprisingly, after sharing the three steps with you, we find that we have three things left to say. The first has to do with the results that you should hope for and expect in your family. The second concerns the big picture, those changes that we hope can occur in America as we work to strengthen our families and as we recognize the family as one of the basic institutions in our society. Finally, we'd like to share some personal thoughts about how fast our time with our children passes and how important it is to take advantage of each day we share with them.

The Proof Is in the Program

Please know, as you struggle with your family laws, your economy, and your traditions, how much we have struggled with ours. We cannot tell you the number of times we have felt that what we were doing was thankless and ineffectual as we heard things like "Oh, no, not 'family time'. . . again!" or "Thanks, but I'd rather be with my friends," or "Don't you think we have enough to memorize in school?" or "This is your dumbest idea yet," or even "Why don't you just leave me alone?" from our children.

For years we just tried to have faith that someday, somewhere, the lessons we hoped we were teaching our children would help them. We made progress, but it was slow and uneven. There were great moments, but there were also times when we felt as if everything we did was unproductive. As we thought back, we could see that we were better off with the three steps than we would have been without them. But in terms of the ups and downs of everyday life, it was impossible to measure just how much difference they had made.

Years did pass, and the older children left for college and other pursuits. Now, as we finish this book, four of our children have started to write back to us about their childhood, helping us to improve our perspective on the three steps and helping us to measure just how effective they were. One child, Saydi, is in her first year of college, while the other three have chosen to take a break from their studies for humanitarian service and missionary work. Our daughter Saren is in Bulgaria, Shawni is in Romania, and Josh is in England.

Their lives, like ours, are not perfect, but their letters home are among the most precious things in our lives. They also provide valuable evidence that the hard work we did with them had results, which motivates us to keep trying with the other five children.

For example we both smiled when we got our very first letter from our brand-new college freshman—who could hardly wait to get away from home.

Oh—I MISS YOU! Thanks so much for the package. Those cookies totally hit the spot! They were so good! I am getting a little sick of the food here. I can't wait to come home and eat the best food in the world—made in our own kitchen. Every day I realize more and more how many things you did for me that I completely took for granted. You're all so wonderful. I don't deserve you. You are the greatest ever.

Love,
Saydi

From Romania comes this wisdom:

I understand more and more each day the importance of the family as I see how it affects people's lives. The family is such an amazing base and foundation—a pattern for good and right. In America it seems that so often the family is treated as so unimportant. The media has made it so that the morally unacceptable is becoming totally acceptable. The scariest thing is what I read the other day about the gradual normalization of aberration. These gentle Romanian people are so good—so innocent without the barrage of media that we are used to. The happiest people, even though they have absolutely nothing in terms of worldly possessions, are the ones with strong families. I'm so grateful for all of our crazy family. Send me those quotes about "stepping out into darkness" and the Shakespeare one about the toad! A couple of those phrases have slipped my mind and I want to put them up on our refrigerator!

Love,
Shawni

We giggled at the following letter from our daughter in Bulgaria, who had left feeling desperate for some privacy

—and quite certain that she was right about nearly every-thing.

I love you all sooooo much! Every time I think about you guys, I feel like my heart is about to burst with joy. Every one of you has taught me so much!

[She goes on to elaborate what she has learned from each member of the family—a wonderful revelation to those who thought they had been quite a lot of trouble to her.]

Well, Mom, here I am in the middle of nowhere, just like you said, wishing I had practiced the piano more. When I go to Sunday meetings, I am the only one who can even read the melody to get us through a hymn!

Service is truly the key to happiness in life. I love the or-phanages. The babies with birth defects need so much love and have so little. When we first came they shrank in fear at our touch. They stay in their dirty little cribs all day with only cockroaches to play with. I love to hold them close and play music to them and see their heads move in time to the music. I love the beautiful little girl with the misshapen head due to an inoperable brain tumor who clings to me, the little boy who is so stiff and sweaty and smiles in surprise at my touch and the baby with the huge blue eyes and uselessly little paralyzed legs who loves music. I want them to know that someone loves them and that sometime in their short little lives someone held them close and made them feel like a precious, real person. Maybe someday, if I'm really really good, I can be friends with those precious spirits in heaven.

Love,
Saren

From London came this surprising revelation from a shy child who has really struggled with communicating verbally:

My companion is very shy and so I have to be the one to get involved with talking to people at their doors and on the street. I thought I hated doing those weird speeches at dinner, but maybe they were O.K. after all. It sure helps me to think on my feet!

By the way, when you get to the part on traditions (in the book you're writing) here's some input from me:

The memories I have from our family traditions is something I wouldn't trade for anything. When I think back on all the things we did together as a family, I cry because I miss and love them so much. Our family traditions have bonded us together better than anything.

When I think about our family traditions, the first one that always comes to mind is our Easter tradition. Every Easter we drive down to Lake Powell and rent a houseboat for a few days. We take morning hikes together up the beautiful canyons, climb the mountains, swim, listen to the song Big River over and over, have barbecues, and play games together after dark every night. Mom always brings a book and reads right before we go to bed every night. Those trips to Lake Powell were some of the greatest times of my life. I also love our Christmas traditions. On Christmas Eve we have a "Nazareth Supper" and act out the first Christmas. Then we give out our presents to our brothers and sisters. We get up at about 3:00 or 4:00 in the morning to look through our stockings, which Santa Claus brought into our rooms at night. At about 7:00 we sing Christmas songs on the stair to wake up Mom and Dad, then we go into the living room to see what Santa brought us and open other presents. We always have Eggs Benedict for breakfast. One of the funniest things we do on Christmas Eve is have a family basketball game. Christmas is such a special time for families. Thanksgiving is also really great. And I loved all our different traditions. I'll never forget them.

Our First Sunday testimonials were really spiritual. I'll never forget them and I'm sure I'll do them with my family.

I loved going on Mommy and Daddy dates. I just wish I would have taken them on more before going on my mission. They really helped our relationships. I would look forward to Sunday Awards, especially when I had done something to earn a particular award, and had a chance to win it. I didn't realize how important Sunday Sessions were at the time I did them when I was little, but now I know it's so important and I'll do it all my life.

Devotional early in the morning was not one of my favorites, but I'm really glad we did it. The scriptures are so important, and we learned some of the greatest quotes. I'll never forget those early morning, sleepy-eyed devotionals. I loved the things we did at dinner time. They livened up our time at the table. We learned a lot about each other.

I love all of our family traditions, and I'll never forget them. I can't wait to do some of them again after I get back home. Traditions really strengthen families.

Love,

Josh

And again from Romania:

Oh I got the best pictures in the mail from you guys this week. I swear everyone has grown a foot. Why are you guys grow-

ing up without me? You guys are the teeniest family now. I hope you are jumping in the leaves an extra lot just for me today and I hope that Dad had a great birthday and that you are all decided on what to be for Halloween.

I hope the book is going great—I am so sorry that I haven't had more time to write for it. I just want to say one thing— nothing a family could ever do could help more than the stuff we did—whenever I give a talk or talk to some random person on the street, I feel so thankful for our little on-the-spot dinner talks. Whenever I talk about prayer I always think about and mention our strong FAMILY prayers—uniting— making our love grow, for each other and for God. Whenever I see a sad or broken family I just wish they could know that if they did more things together it could change their lives. I wish some of these little kids could sit around the dinner table and talk about how they were a "leader for the right," and glow with pride when they realize they "did what Jesus would do." I wish each Romanian mom or dad, when walking a child home at night with a loaf of bread under each arm and a couple of bags of potatoes and peppers, would bend down and say, "Hey, this is sort of like a date (a Mommy/daddy date!). I love being with you!"

I wish every family had family traditions that warm up their whole hearts and unite them—I wish every family would take time even once a month and sit together and say how much they love each other and love life. Things like this could change the world. The family is the eternal unit—if families are strong nations will be strong. The family is the building block. Oh how I love you all. Write a lot!

Love,
Shawni

227

As we said, our children's letters are among the most precious things we have. They remind us of what our hard work and sacrifices were for, and stand as evidence of the results. We like to think that the rules, responsibilities, and traditions in the three steps were an important part of keeping our family strong and happy. We hope that they'll continue to work for us and for you.

The Big Picture

Besides the personal, family, and individual benefits of the three steps, we can enjoy a huge society-wide benefit from strengthening our families. It is the only way we can solve this nation's social problems. America's social problems rival the former Soviet Union's economic problems in their scope and seriousness—and in their potential eventually to bring our country to its knees.

When problems are not solved within a nation's families, when good citizens are not produced in its homes, when irresponsible, valueless behavior spills out of society's most basic institution into the larger institutions of schools and governments, it becomes nearly impossible to stop. These problems endanger our streets, corrupt our institutions, raise our taxes, destroy our potential, and rob us of our collective security and idealism.

So while the first reason for building a strong family is the happiness and security it gives to children, and the time and stress it saves for parents, the second reason is that strong families are our only guarantee of a strong society. Children from solid, functional families grow up and create solid, functional families of their own.

America's social problems can only be solved within America's families. This becomes apparent when we contemplate how the family fits into a diagram showing the major divisions of society:

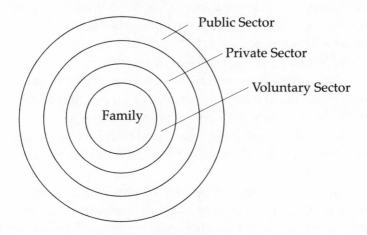

The bull's-eye in this diagram represents the family. The next "ring" represents the voluntary sector (churches, community organizations, scouting, etc.), which exists primarily to strengthen and support families. The third ring is the private sector, which supplies families with their livelihood and more and more tries to help with the social and personal needs of employees. The outer ring is the public sector. Ideally this should be the thinnest ring, dealing only with problems that cannot be met by the family, voluntary, or private sector. If the family fails, the role of the other sectors broaden as social problems mushroom. In society today unfortunately the public sector has grown more and more swollen as we attempt to deal with the societal crises that are the result of weak or dysfunctional families.

229

I've been in and out of the public and private sectors all my life. I directed a White House conference, worked for a U.S. Senator, and ran for governor. I've been a management consultant, founded businesses, and worked for big corporations. The longer I work and the more I see, the more I'm convinced that neither the public nor the private sectors will provide answers or solutions for society's problems.

The full range of social ills—extending from homelessness to welfare, from drugs to juvenile crime and teen pregnancy, from pollution to inner-city blight, from learning readiness to public education, even from international competitiveness to economic stagnation—can't be solved by businesses and governments because their roots lie elsewhere—in homes and families.

Now I devote what time and energy I have to the two inner sectors of the diagram—family and volunteerism. Besides working on books about the family and family organizations, I serve on the board of the National Volunteer Center, consult for the Points of Light Foundation, and try to set up things such as sister cities and family-to-family interventions.

What we need in America is less government and more volunteerism, fewer substitutes and more support for the family, less emphasis on quantity (materialism) and more on quality (simplicity and relationships).

—Richard

Abraham Lincoln said, "If America is ever to be destroyed, it will not be from without, it will be from within." Now, 140 years later, we see that internal destruction of values, of responsibility, of self-reliance, and of families—

and we must say to ourselves, "If America is ever to be saved, it will be from within—within our homes."

Strong families are America's last, best hope. Parents are the keepers of the flame. What matters most is not what happens in Congress or in the White House but what happens in communities and in your house.

Making Every Day Count

I hadn't seen him for two years. Uncle Cyril, my dad's closest brother, once so vigorous and agile, now in the grasp of time after ninety years. We had come for a short family vacation to Idaho—to a lake near where Cyril lived, partly so that I could see him one more time. The same smile was there that I remembered from my childhood, but more wrinkled; the same skin but now speckled with age and almost transparent; the same body but stiff, shrinking, and fragile; and most especially the same wonderful dry wit and clever mind, which was now only semiclear.

We talked for an hour in a living room filled with memorabilia—wedding pictures, portraits, and snapshots of children and grandchildren. Uncle Cyril even played a couple of shaky but familiar tunes on his little organ and puffed out a favorite hymn on his harmonica before he became exhausted and gasped for breath in an uncontrollable spasm.

Soon he regained his composure, and we talked about his childhood, especially about the things he could remember about his parents and the great times he had with my dad and the poignant moments he remembered from the distant past as if they were yesterday.

Just being in the house brought back memories of my own life as a child and the fun romps I had with his children, my cousins, and the good food Aunt Gladys had prepared for us there—and of my own dear father already ten years gone and so much like this wonderful man. In my mind I was a little girl again.

After bidding a fond farewell, which I knew might be my last, I spent the half hour riding back to the lake wondering what memories my children will have of me when I am ninety—when all of those days of perpetual picking up and practicing and arguing about whether or not to have breakfast cereal for lunch and dinner are over.

Will my children remember my irritation at two-year-old messes, or my tantrums when a child lost his orthodontic headgear—again? Or will they remember my reading them stories or playing the occasional tennis matches?

Which will they remember best: feeling angry with me for an unfair judgment or laughing at me and my hysterically hopeless efforts to drop a water ski and slalom?

What will they remember hearing most? "Practice," "Be sure that you're in by midnight," "Get in the car, we're late"? Or "There isn't anything you can't do if you set your mind to it," and "I love you more than you can possibly understand"?

Will they remember me always rushing off to meet the next deadline, or will they remember the long talks after midnight?

Still deep in thought, I pulled up in front of our little summer lakeside cabin, slipped inside unnoticed, and began fixing dinner. Before five minutes had passed, our ten-year-old, Talmadge, came and put his hand on my shoulder and said, "Mom, come out to the raft with us. It's so hot, and the water is so cool. You could watch me dive. I've got a great new trick to show you!"

"You go down there, and I'll be there as soon as I get this into the oven," I said.

"Oh, Mom, c'mon" was his response. "You always say that, but you hardly ever make it down to the water."

I looked into the pleading eyes of this child who was ten years old, five months, and twenty-one days old—for only one day in his whole life—and came to my senses.

"You know what?" I said. "I'm coming right this minute. Dinner can wait . . . because pretty soon you'll be gone and I'll be ninety." He looked confused, but happy.

—Linda

Our time with our children while they are young is as fleeting as a beautiful sunset. They'll be gone before we know it, and if we don't take the time to really look at them, communicate with them, and give them the security they need, we'll be left thinking, *If only . . .*

Yes, it does take time to implement the three steps and produce results, but every hour spent is a great investment in your children's confidence and sense of well-being—not only for next year but for a lifetime and for what comes after.

Thanks for reading. Thanks for listening. Thanks for thinking about and caring about your children. All parents, regardless of how much their circumstances vary, share a great common bond through their love for their children and the challenge of being good parents and balanced individuals in a complex, difficult world. As parents we feel that bond with you and hope to stay in touch. Send your feedback and ideas to us at the HOMEBASE address given at the end of the book. Let's help each other, let's pray for each other. Let's save the world and its values—one family at a time.

All the best,

Linda and

Richard

Homebase

Okay, you've taken the three steps . . . or you're starting on them . . . or you're thinking about them . . . or you've read about them.

What now?

Just do it!

Then what?

How do you stick with it, keep it exciting and interesting, stay motivated?

HOMEBASE is an international parenting organization that sends out a monthly newsletter and has four parenting programs: *Joy School* for preschoolers; *TCR* (Teaching Children Responsibility) for elementary age; *TCV* (Teaching Children Values) for all ages, but especially adolescents; and *Lifebalance* for too-busy parents who need some simplifying and harmony. Each program includes monthly workbooks, tapes, and a newsletter.

Call (801) 581-0112 for a membership catalog and an introductory audiotape (or clip and send in the coupon on page 237).

To obtain a free catalog of HOMEBASE parenting and family programs and an overview audiotape by Richard and Linda Eyre, send $5.00 for postage and handling with the card below to:

HOMEBASE
1615 South Foothill Drive
Salt Lake City, UT 84108
or call (801) 581-0112

HOMEBASE

. . . is an international co-op of parents dedicated to making children and family their first priority and to the fostering of traditional values and correct principles in all of our institutions and in society at large.

Yes! I am interested in the possibility of membership in HOMEBASE. Please send me further information about:

☐ TCJ ☐ TCV
☐ TCR ☐ LFB

For preschoolers "TCJ" (Teaching Children Joy) or "Joy Schools" - In-home, do-it-yourself neighborhood preschools focusing on the physical, mental and social "joys" of childhood.

For elementary age children "TCR" (Teaching Children Responsibility) - A program (stories, discussions, music) to conduct around the dinner table that teaches all forms of responsibility and self reliance.

For all ages but particularly adolescents "TCV" (Teaching Children Values) - A once-a-week Sunday program — materials and audio tapes to teach sensitivity, honesty and other values.

For busy parents "LFB" (Lifebalance) - A video and audio tape seminar with fill-in-the blank materials on how to balance family, work and personal needs.

Name _____

Address _____

street _____

Phone _____
area code / number

city / state / zip